BARONET

# CZECHS
# AND
# BALANCES:
## a nation's survival kit

PRAHA 1998

Benjamin Kuras: CZECHS AND BALANCES:
a nation's survival kit
Copyright © 1996, 1998 Benjamin Kuras
All rights reserved.

Vydalo nakladatelství Baronet a. s., Široká 22, Praha 1
v roce 1998 jako svou 349. publikaci.
Vydání druhé.
Kresba na obálce © 1996, 1998 Zdeněk Mézl
Ilustrace © 1996, 1998 Zdeněk Mézl
Sazba, grafická úprava a obálka studio Ricardo, Sudoměřská 32, Praha 3.
Vytiskla a svázala Tiskárna MV p.o., Bartůňkova 4, Praha 4.

Název a logo BARONET je ochranná známka, která je zapsána do rejstříku
ochranných známek Úřadu průmyslového vlastnictví pod číslem zápisu 189296.

ISBN 80-7214-136-8

BARONET
PRAHA 1998

# BENJAMIN KURAS

# CZECHS AND BALANCES:

## a nation's survival kit

**BARONET**

*Special thanks to Ladislav Venyš
for suggesting the idea in the first place,
flogging me into writing it, and caringly
preparing it for publication. To Richard Carlyon
and Therese Buchmeier for their patient
and meticulous editing and proofreading,
and additional ideas.*

# I.

# The Czechs' Bouncing Tools

# Worship

"The Czechs," says English kabbalist Z'ev ben Shimon Halevi, "have always worshipped three things: women, food, and God – in that order."

Anyone who has made more than a passing acquaintance with the Czechs will surely recognise this to be a very accurate observation. As they grow older and wiser, however, the Czechs restructure their worship priorities in reverse order: food, women, and God.

Czech women, on the other hand, somehow miraculously manage to make their male chauvinist pigs believe that they worship one thing, and one thing alone: them. Which may explain why post-communist Prague has become the home of some thirty thousand young horny and affection-starved American males.

And let's face it, boys. Where else do you find a beautifully feminine, gentle, sexy and caring female with a university degree who takes you lovingly into her home, gives you breakfast in bed, irons your shirts, goes off to work smartly dressed, comes home to you cheerful and unaffected by stress, cooks you dinner, massages you from head to toe, bonks you blind, blows you back up for another round when you thought you were finished for a week, does not get tired, does not fake orgasm, keeps telling you how wonderful you are, and does not want to change you – and manages to be all that on an average income of 200 dollars a month?

\*\*\*

# Flexible history

It is often said that nations, their characteristics, temperaments, aspirations, and degrees of success or failure, are the result of their history. It is, in fact, the other way around. Most nations' histories consist partly of legends and myths, partly of biased interpretation of some actually documented and some putative historical events, but mainly of a current consensus to view the collective past in a way which would assist in the creation of a particular model of the future. History has always been the result of people's decisions about actions to be taken. Those, in turn, are determined by the image people have of their past at the time they are deciding. Rewriting history to one's image in order to change one's future is a legitimate tool of national survival.

This is something of which the Czechs should be particularly well aware, having in one lifetime come to see and accept themselves variously as:

a) the economic backbone of the Austro-Hungarian Empire without whose protection, however, they would not have been able to survive (they did),

b) exemplary Western-style democrats of great strategic value to the great democracies of the West (ditched),

c) a bridge between East and West (walked over),

d) humanist socialists who would adapt Marxism to democratic European traditions (for a couple of years prior and a couple of hours following peaceful power hand-over to communists),

e) socialists with a human face (a large basketful of eggs thrown into it),

f) the most enterprising and westernised of the ex-communist nations (one side of the current post-communist image's coin), and

g) wishy-washy morally bent and corrupt artful dodgers (the other side of the current post-communist image's coin).

This book looks at some of the Czechs' historical myths and legends and the type of events they precipitated. It tries to debunk some of the myths Czechs live by unconsciously or unwittingly as they approach the turn of the millennium. And it looks at other possible interpretations of the myths, which could produce different results. Just in case the Czechs should decide one day that different results are what they want.

At no point does the book pretend it is presenting an accurate or even reasonably approximate account of historical events. It contents itself with being as biased as every other view of Czech history has been so far and is ever likely to be.

The purpose of this particular bias is not to assist Czechs in creating a particular type of future. Nor is it to assist others in viewing the Czechs in a friendlier (or more hostile) manner than they would otherwise.

The single purpose of this book is to squeeze some drama and fun out of what has always been presented to the Czechs themselves as so dull and uninteresting that it comes as no surprise or embarrassment to them that they know less of their history than English businessmen and engineers who are trying to expiate for Munich by attempting to do straight and fair business with Czech companies and officials in competition with the shrewder and more knowing-whom-to-bribe Germans.

True, the dullness of their history may have been deliberately devised by various occupying powers, with a defined purpose: To obliterate the nation's self-respect and awareness of its political importance, spiritual and moral strength, military prowess, cultural achievement, economic skills, and sense of glory. But it cuts so deep into the Czech psyche that turning it around might take more than one generation of sustained material success, national *chutzpeh*, and an occasional friendly nudge from the established good and great. Whoever decides to do some of the friendly nudging will benefit severalfold, for Czechs like to go out of their way to please those who have been good to them, and even those who they think might be.

*** 

## The invincible consonant

An early health warning: If you think you can ever come to grips with a people who can converse without vowels, you have another think coming.

The bonk you had a few pages back is called *mrd*. Which is just one of about thirty words the Czechs have for love-making, depending on the way it is done, speed and duration, the attitude with which it is approached, state of mind, and depth of emotional involvement. A *mrd* would be a hearty down to earth, athletic rather than tender, with full abandon and lot of yelling, no-nonsense and let's-get-on-with-it approach, not worrying too much about emotional depth of involvement but mutually satisfying, ending in healthy fatigue and a good night's sleep. Another one would be *hrk*, which is a giggly friendly quickie with someone you are familiar enough with not to have to waste time on foreplay every time. A *drb* is an uninvolved, absent-minded, cynical and loveless act, taking no account of your partner's feelings, sort of rabbit-like. All other ways have some vowels, as an expression of something smoother, rounder, gentler, slower, longer, more thoughtful, or more delicious.

If you cannot tell one way from another, you are a *blb*, which is the most frequent Czech word for idiot. If you were not an idiot before but have just become one, the verb participle would be *zblbl*.

The male organ used for the *hrk* is a *brk*, and the jerky motion in which it is done is a *strk*. The finger used

13

for the foreplay with is *prst*, and the breast it started on was *prs*.

If you were moved to ecstasy, your eyes could weep with a lot of *slz*, and you could be proud of yourself – or *hrd*.

The forest you did it in was a *brd*, and the pebbles on the beech were *drt́*.

The gulp of beer you had afterwards was *hlt,* and if you have just gulped some, *zhltl* is what you have done in Czech. A very hearty *hlt* is a *glg*, and the belch which follows it is *krk*. *Krk* is also the throat down which you poured your beer, while *smrt* is the death you die if someone throttles you or gives you a *škrt*. The same *škrt* can also mean deletion or budget cut, if that's what you prefer.

If someone wants to resuscitate you by splashing some water over you, he would give you a *chrst*. And what the man who splashed the water into your face did was *vchrstl*.

Are you sure you still want to get to know these extra-terrestrials?

\*\*\*

### Bounce-back

The way nations behave is directly related to the way they view themselves and their history. Similarly, the way in which they are behaved towards is related to the way in which they and their history are viewed by their neighbours. That in turn depends on how they allow their neighbours to view them and treat them. No one with a modicum of historical awareness could have failed to notice the dramatic change in the psyche of the lethargic Brits following Churchill's "blood, sweat, and tears", or in the survival determination of the Jews following the new State of Israel's proclamation "never again a Jew murdered with impunity for being a Jew".

In a nutshell – a nation is what a decisive majority of its members is determined to be. The absence of a clear determination to be anything clearly identifiable and worth defending, and the absence of historical myths which would give such determination the necessary psychological back-up, is a guaranteed recipe for a nation's demise from history, its absorption into another more determined neighbouring nation, and cultural and political, if not physical, annihilation.

The Czechs have been on the verge of it several times. The very fact they are still around today – after even the omniscient Karl Marx predicted their disappearance by the end of the nineteenth century – indicates a resilience, a bounce-back, pick-up, and dust-off power which seems to emerge out of nowhere to everyone's surprise each time it does.

Reichsprotektor Reinhard Heydrich, when briefing his Prague gestapo chiefs, is quoted as warning them that while Poles and Yugoslavs were tough and stiff and easily broken by a strong enough force, the Czechs were spineless flexible twigs that bent down under pressure, only to lash back when least expected. Right he was, too, and off he went with the least expected lashback by a couple of London-run Czech paratroopers at a time when Czech resistance seemed pacified by an extra tin of sardines for a good day's work in their arms and ammunition factories.

In 1993, with Slovakia going its own proud if somewhat precarious way, the Czechs were given a unique opportunity – for the first time in over five centuries – to find out who they are and work out who they want to be – on their own. What they find out, and what they work out, will depend to a decisive degree on which of their historical myths they decide to dig out, enlarge, pin up, and live by.

***

## The milky goat

The lukewarm attitude most Czechs have to their own religion – insofar as they can be bothered to adhere to one – could explain why religious differences figure so low on the scale of the Czechs' prejudices. Far more interesting – and right at the top – is envy of anyone else's success.

No significant religiously motivated hostilities have turned Czech against Czech since the Thirty Year War. But deeply ingrained dislike and profound mistrust of anyone who has done even a notch better was no doubt the decisive factor that threw this otherwise profoundly democratic, humanist, individualist, and not readily hoodwinkable people into the communist embrace for two generations. It is what motivates another generation of fledgling capitalists to settle their business disputes through hired assassins dumping competitors into lakes with iron slabs chained to their necks. Or chopping them up and marinating them in brine-filled casks. To mention just two of the more sophisticated and increasingly popular well-documented business strategies.

All these are not much more than an ever so slightly amplified version of a traditional Czech joke, which goes like this:

A fairy-tale old magician appears to a Frenchman, an Englishman, and a Czech, with an offer to fulfill for each of them one secret wish. The Frenchman recalls recently meeting a most attractive woman engaged to a former schoolmate of his. His wish is to have her for just one night before she marries his schoolmate. The Englishman asks for a replica of Lord Brondesbury's ivory pipe, making sure His Lordship should retain his original for everyone to notice both. The Czech mentions a very healthy-looking and milk-rich goat owned by his next door neighbour. "You want one just like his?" asks the magician. "No, sir," replies the Czech, "I want his goat to drop dead."

Not even greed and envy can motivate Czechs to surrender to the evil forces of Mammon.

*** 

## Flagellation

Few nations spend so much time and intellectual energy brooding on their national characteristics, purpose, role, destiny, meaning of existence, image, and self-image, as do the Czechs. Few nations brooding about their existence are so consistently wrong in their conclusions. And probably no nation in recorded history has viewed itself so much more harshly than it is viewed by others. To a detached but concerned observer, the Czechs' persistent self-reflection looks like self-flagellation. And yet, there are too many Czechs – mostly among intellectuals – who believe they have had nowhere near enough flogging yet.

Foremost among the national floggers are Czech journalists who have a particular flair for uncovering some obnoxious national vice or other behind every mistake or misdeed committed by just about anyone from government officials, parliament members, and representatives of all levels of officialdom, to members of opposition, ex-communists (repented or die-hard), ex-dissidents (promoted to officialdom or consigned to oblivion), ex-non-communist-non-dissidents, drivers, pedestrians, orchestra musicians, ex-theatre-goers turned television-gogglers, readers of a particular newspaper, non-readers of a particular newspaper, and – above all – other journalists. No wonder the Czech Prime Minister publicly reviles journalists as the most detestable breed of people ever to walk this planet.

"With people like us, behaving as we do, we cannot ever dream of being accepted by Europe, nor do we deserve to" – is a popular flog in the Czech intellectuals' repertory, and the most likely one to be heeded when all other flogs have failed. By the time Europe decides to embrace the Czechs – which experts believe is likely to be seriously contemplated, as opposed to just blabbered about, around the year 2005 – the Czechs will have surely flogged themselves into being more European than the Europeans. Whether they can be expected to stop flogging themselves then is another matter, one Europe should seriously ponder before taking them in without first introducing some anti-self-flogging directives.

There is, however, a redeeming feature to Czech flagellation. Unlike the Poles – whose historic mission is to flog themselves for Europe, or the Russians – who flog themselves (and the odd neighbour or two) for mankind's salvation, the Czechs do most of their flogging for the sheer hell of it.

\*\*\*

## Wisdom of inadequacy

The characteristics of every nation – be they home-spun or externally perceived – are always a mix of positive and negative features. The only exception are the Americans, who have no home-spun negative features whatsoever. Which explains why they are so deeply loved wherever they go.

What a home-spun image sees as positive may be seen as negative by outsiders, and vice versa. Nations may even be split into bellicose camps who regard the same feature as positive and negative respectively. Whatever other disagreements they might have, Czechs are remarkably united in regarding themselves as the most inadequate and undeserving lot on this planet one day, and exceptionally enlightened bearers of state-of-the-art wisdom to the world if only the world would care to listen on another day. This wonderful blend becomes more appreciable once we notice that the inadequate lot are always all Czechs except us, while the wisdom-bearers are always us rather than the other Czechs. Unless, of course, the other Czechs are inadequate wisdom-bearers and, as such, a national embarrassment no matter how popular they may be abroad.

The Czech intellectual elite has always had a recognisable tendency to elevate inadequacy to a national virtue, and even regard it as the nation's specific strength with which "the adequate" can be outsmarted and overpowered – and if not that, then surely at least outnumbered.

This applies particularly during the rule of morally unacceptable regimes when – to quote a famous Czech comedy actor – "it is immoral to pursue a successful career under an immoral regime". Since most Czechs have always regarded most of their governments as immoral, they tend to view as crooked anyone who succeeds at anything at just about any time.

One thing that does not seem to have occurred to the Czechs when trying to live up to the famous comedy actor's adage was to ponder how he could have become a famous comedy actor without pursuing a successful career. But taking the micky out of nations is what comedy actors are here for. So, of course, are politicians, most of whom, if sincerely questioned, would admit that deep down they really are frustrated comedians.

Czechs don't exert adequate effort to replace their immoral governments with ones that might be more moral because they believe that the alternative would be at least as bad and probably worse. The logic is that no morally clean politician can ever be adequate, for in order to gain adequate political experience and skills, he would have had to pursue a successful career under an immoral regime, and could therefore not be morally clean if he had found it appropriate to do so.

If a morally clean person does, by some stroke of luck, succeed to a position of power, he will be suspected of having made some immoral pact with the immoral, or at best, of being manipulated by the immoral into fooling the public that there might be something moral going on after all, and must therefore be quite thick – or at best inadequate (i.e. one of us) – yet another national embarrassment. Even if he is found to have been morally clean before he took office, he will have become unclean by the time the findings are completed.

***

## The art of embarrassment

Embarrassment is one the Czechs' favourite arts. And masters of it they are, too. From early childhood – at home as well as at school – Czechs receive a thorough training from their elders in how to create embarrassing situations for others. This is done by persistent coaching from parents and teachers, which entails frequent repetition of a simple command: "Don't you dare make an asshole of yourself or your family (group, club, town, nation, etc.)".

This has taught Czechs something they have become very skilled at – image building. They take pains, and very often succeed, to present themselves to the outside world in a much better light than they see themselves. This they do by not exactly lying about themselves, just being economical with the truth. Censoring the facts ever so slightly. Harmless, really. Underneath, nothing is ever as good as it looks packaged for foreign consumption. Giving his country (family, group, town, etc.) a bad image – i.e. embarrassing it – is the worst offence a Czech could commit in the eyes of his fellows.

Since making an asshole of himself – i.e. creating embarrassment – is part of any child's natural instinct and an inalienable right, Czech children soon learn the trick of making assholes of others and other families (other groups, other clubs, other towns, other nations, etc.), and get a lot of fun out of it.

Since they were not at the same time taught the skill of gracefully sailing out of an embarrassing situation someone else has brought them (being a landlocked nation), the only defence available to them is to drag the opponent into an even greater embarrassment. To which, of course, he can only respond by creating yet a greater embarrassment for them. The most remarkable display of the mastery of this art can be seen in Czech TV debates in which public figures participate not so much to discuss an idea and argue its worth – but to make the greatest possible assholes of their opponents.

Some Czech leading figures like to apply this technique even outside the country on innocent, untrained and unsuspecting audiences. Having clearly conveyed the unambiguous message, "You, sir\madam, are an asshole", to everyone who asked a question, they come back home surprised at how distorted the reports of their visit were, and how much less goodwill they had created than intended. It must surely be those goddamned asshole journalists again.

Other Czech public figures then wallow in the bliss

of seeing these Czech public figures making assholes of themselves abroad and being an embarrassment to the nation. And so the art of embarrassment flourishes.

How the Slovaks could have ever made any sense out of living with the Czechs is a mystery worth serious historical and psychological analysis. They probably need years of psychotherapy to recover. Even more mysterious – to the point of being a case for psychiatrists – is why Sudeten Germans, having for two generations been so blissfully free of the Czechs, should now want to return to live in their midst again. Plain nuts. Unless, of course, they are after the women, like everyone else.

***

## Comfort

The Czechs love their comfort. So much so that their comfort considerations usually overrule such hollow concepts as ideology, idealism, heroism, honour, gallantry – and sometimes even less hollow ones like duty, loyalty, honesty, ethics, reliability. Which does not make them a dishonest, unethical, or unreliable people, without any sense of duty and loyalty. They can be very loyal, committed, and even deeply devoted to their comfort. Anyone demanding their loyalty would first have to guarantee them their comfort.

This was well understood by wartime Nazi occupation authorities who took great pains not to subject the Czechs to such harsh discomfort as they did the Poles, the Serbs, the Greeks, or the Russians. For this, the Czechs rewarded the Nazis by not making too much trouble for them.

This joke, which the Czechs don't like hearing too much, was probably made up by a Slovak:

A Czech and a Yugoslav meet after the war and discuss their war-time experiences.

"Whenever we saw a German in uniform, we'd cut his throat," says the Yugoslav matter-of-factly.

Replies the Czech:

"You know, we would have liked to do it too, but in our country, that was not allowed".

The Czechs' craving for comfort was best understood by the communist regime which made life for them dull and idiotic, but compared with the rest of the communist world, remarkably comfortable. There was hardly a family which had not built itself a second home in the country to escape to every weekend – starting at midday on Friday and ending at midday on Monday.

When the iron curtain crumbled and Czech "capitalist" expatriates visited their erstwhile homeland for the first time in many years, they could not hold their amazement at how much more comfortable their homeland friends were than they themselves in the affluent West. Not richer, but more comfortable. Enjoying more comfort at much lower cost and with much less effort. And taking it for granted, too. They still do – and are wondering now what exactly it is that anyone from the West can teach them that they are not better at – as far as creation of comfort is concerned. For it is the creation of comfort, isn't it, that is the sole purpose of any human endeavour? Surely? Well, isn't it?

The endlessly used Czech word for comfort – *pohoda* – means a great deal more than mere physical comfort. It also means hominess, coziness, harmony, self-satisfaction, easy-going relationships, rewarding and not too strenuous activity, pleasant overall atmosphere, absence of strife, effort or pain, an undisturbed pastoral idyll. It means a state of affairs which involves no need to take risks or face challenges, be disturbed by new or unfamiliar things, have to deal with dangers or shortages.

This does not make Czechs a very adventurous people. It makes them an inventive and purposefully creative if sometimes irritatingly procrastinating lot, slowly but steadily and reliably working their way out of discomfort towards the greatest possible comfort that looks achievable, while eschewing any discomfort on the way. Thus, they may sometimes satisfy themselves with medium comfort if the achievement of a greater comfort involves – or even is perceived to involve – too much discomfort. The flagellants like to call this "wallowing in mediocrity".

But it was to his beloved Czechs that Bruce Lockhart broadcast from London in 1948: "A country which prefers comfort and tranquility to freedom will lose its freedom and with it, ironically, its comfort and tranquility as well."

As someone who tries to avoid physical pain at all cost, a Czech cannot easily be motivated to inflict physical pain even on his worst enemies. Slow, gradual, and hardly noticeable mental torture, frequently masked as comfort, is always considered the better option in his hierarchy of weapons.

*Pohoda* is also the state of mind in which Czechs like to do their work, provide a service, do a favour. If they are satisfied that what you are asking them to do can be done easily and without much risk of failure, they will tell you they can do it *"v pohodě"*. This means literally in comfort, though a more accurate translation would probably be the more colloquial "no sweat".

The somewhat earthier Moravians with their more florid, kinesthetically and olfactorily opulent usage of the Czech language, would perform an easy task for

24

you not just in comfort, not even just standing on their heads, but with both hands in their arsehole.

More on them later.

*\*\**

## Atheism and ideological indifference

An unstoppable flood of Czechs returning to the Catholic faith was expected by the Church and its devout believers after the collapse of communism. Naively, as it turned out. The nation was believed to be yearning for the Church's guiding hand following forty years of godless tyranny. Naively again. They were, after all, still believed to be at least seventy five percent Catholic, as they had been registered before communism took power and forced everyone who wanted to hang on to a decent job to declare himself officially "of no faith". For the sake of comfort, most did. To those few who didn't, various degrees of discomfort were meted out – from no job promotion if they were professionally indispensable to landing in labour camps if they weren't, and every imaginable degree in between.

The Church's hopes went awry when all three avowedly Christian parties together failed to get even ten percent of the nation's vote in the first election, in spite of the plainly visible fact that none of the other parties declared themselves even knowledgeable, let alone supportive, of anything that might smack of religious values. A return of strayed sheep to the Church's flock failed to take place. The Czechs obviously did not feel convinced that organised religion was capable of, or even interested in, providing more comfort, and decided to do without ideologies altogether and be guided solely by the most humane of ethics – desire for their own comfort. For this, the post-communist government was perceived to provide the best framework. In every survey since then, Czechs have figured as statistically the least religious nation in Europe.

The reason for this could probably be found in their history, during which they were forced to switch ideological allegiances time and time again, always for the same single reason: to avoid discomfort. Czech ideological and religious history in a nutshell goes as follows:

## 1. Celts and pagans

Celtic Christianity of St. Patrick's mission from Ireland some time in the 6th century, among what was at the time probably still a fairly mixed population of Celts and Slav-speaking Moravians, with a smattering of some Germanic tribes. No record of St. Patrick's local liturgy or literature. No practicing survivors, though some may have emigrated to Ireland since. This meek religion tries to compete with the then popular Czech pagan rite of virile gods like Radegast (now a popular beer) who thunder down the mountain slopes to mate and make merry with the local oh ever-so-lovely maidens.

## 2. Slav Christians

Moravian Greco-Slav rite in the 9th century, with Slav liturgy and bits of Bible translations. Some texts and the alphabet extant for students of Slavonic studies. Practicing survivors pushed eastward to set up what is to become the Russian Orthodox Church, never quite relinquishing their right to return to their cradle, in tanks if need be.

## 3. Roman rite over Slav

Conversion to the Roman Catholic rite in the 10th century, largely carried out by neighbouring German missionaries at the invitation of Wenceslas, the legendary Prince (not King, for the Czechs were only a principality at the time), about whom it is still difficult to decide whether he was an enlightened civiliser or a cowardly quisling.

## 4. Czech Protestantism

Outbreak of Czech national fervent Protestantism following the 1415 burning of popular Prague hippy preacher Jan Hus, who had the outrageous idea of letting his congregants read the Bible in their own language, and had himself provided some of the translation. One of the few great legends of Czech military prowess run by a brilliant strategist, the furious one-eyed south Bohemian squire Jan Žižka. His peasant armies defeat several crusades and keep chasing them all the way across Germany for fifteen years running, burning the odd cathedral or two in passing, and spreading the "wine for everyone, cheers" message to the local soon-to-become Lutherans. Under the banner of the chalice, the Hussites' multi-vocal rendering of "God's Warriors", top of the pops of the day (conveniently used by later Czech composers as an expression of patriotic mood calculated to move Czechs to tears), appeared to have the same effect on the invading crusaders as the Cockney war-stopper mono-testicled Hitler song must have had on the average German soldier's fighting spirit when the Brits marched in behind the bagpipes, singing: *'I'ler 'as only go' one ball, Goerin' s'go' two bu' very small, 'Imler 's go' somefin' simlar, and poor ol' Goeballs 'as no balls a' all.*

## 5. Protestant tolerance

Religious toleration law under King George (Jiří) Podebrad in the mid-1400s, legislating tolerance of Catholics by the then estimated 85% Protestant population, as second best to a failed attempt at establishing an outright Protestant kingdom. For his tolerance of a subversive Catholic minority, George is rewarded with the title of heretic by the Catholic Church. Crusades move on the Czechs again, with active participation of the Hungarians who, having already taken the oh, ever-so-lovely women of Slovakia, are now after the oh, ever-so-lovely women of Moravia and Silesia, which they occupy for one year before being driven back again by Czech military prowess, only to re-occupy them again a few years later, while losing their own land to the Turks, almost causing Central Europe to be converted to Islam by fire and sword.

## 6. Enter the Habsburgs

Czech Kingdom – which still incorporates the whole of Silesia – confederates with Austria and Hungary in 1526 in a joint effort to drive the Turks out of central Europe. Austrian Habsburg kings promptly seize the opportunity to take the Czechs over by marrying onto their throne, thus becoming their hereditary kings. More Catholic pressure follows, as the Austrians slowly but steadily turn their erstwhile confederate partner into an Austrian-run province, with germanisation slowly creeping in.

## 7. Protestant defeat

Defeat of Protestants (mainly Czech but some Germans) by Catholic (international motley but some Czechs) armies at the White Mountain (Bílá Hora) in 1620. This triggers off thirty years of bloody warfare in which the population of the Czech kingdom is halved, its educated Protestant classes exiled – some all the way to England and America to become known as the Moravian Brethren. The remaining decimated and by now predominantly peasant population is promptly and comfortably re-catholicised.

## 8. Fast re-catholicisation

A brave attempt by Protestant Sweden, prompted by exiled Czech Protestants, to liberate the Czech kingdom from Catholic rule and return power to the Protestants, meets with fierce resistance from the by now thoroughly catholicised Czechs who forgot their two centuries of glorious Protestantism in a few years. Sent packing and understandably peeved, the retreating Swedes set out to plunder and steal whatever they can on the way home, including the indigenous Czech word for physician – *lékař*, turned into *lekare*, for which they have failed to come up with their own indigenous alternative to this day.

## 9. Everyone is a Catholic

When bonfires of books start burning in Czech towns and villages, the comfort-loving country folk realise the Church is no joke. Not wanting to become fire fodder themselves, they settle into a cozy, comfortable, cuddly, homey, undisturbed soft and sweet version of bare-bummed little angels, baroque Catholicism which is as far removed from the Austro-German pomposity as the soft Portuguese baroque is from the harsh Spanish one. Underneath the surface of devout Catholicism simmers a folk revival of pagan gods in the form of fairies, mermaids, and gnomes in what becomes one of the richest fairy tale traditions in Europe. Humanising the devil into a chummy cuddly innocent harmless little man who can't even scare children, and carving funny little statues of him, is one of the Czechs' naughty cockasnooks at the Church, with which they just about get away short of being burned as satanists.

## 10. Language revival

By late 18th century, Czech – once a language of rich Renaissance literature and Bible translation – is almost dead and has to be painstakingly reconstructed by linguists and historians who now mostly speak and write better German than their own country dialects. It takes two generations before quality literature is written in Czech again – though today's flagellants would say it still hasn't been. European Enlightenment loosens the Catholic grip and some Czechs begin to return to Protestantism, which they identify with the glory of the pre-Habsburg Czech kingdom. Many more discover a rich new world outside religion altogether, and socialism finds fertile soil in the Czech sod-the-establishment psyche.

## 11. Habsburgs go home

As the Habsburg empire collapses in a lost war, American-style democratic capitalism breaks loose on the Czechs and turns fledgling and ethnically fragile Czechoslovakia into the world's tenth most productive economy. Independent statehood, handed to the Czechs on a silver platter by allied powers, turns them overnight into civic democrats but ethnic autocrats trying to be efficient masters of a country in which they constitute only half of the population. The other half being Germans, Slovaks, Hungarians, Poles, Ruthenians, and of course the long-established and well-assimilated Jews, as well as the ever unassimilable Gipsies – the latter two proving the only loyal ones, suspecting all available alternatives to Czech rule to be worse, as indeed they turned out to be. Thus the Czechs squander a unique chance to become another – and probably richer – Switzerland. An eminent example of the Czech's weakness for taking on a bigger morsel than they can chew.

## 12. Independence lost again

With half of its population proving disloyal in a critical situation, and with its clumsy international diplomacy resulting in Rumania as its only loyal ally, Czechoslovakia disappears from the map. As they gained statehood without a fight, so without a fight the

Czechs lose it again. Three years later, a quarter of a million of them gather in Prague's Wenceslas Square *sieg-heiling* their loyalty to the Reich and demanding severe punishment for Heydrich's assassins and their sympathisers, while singing the Czech national anthem *Where Is My Home*.

## 13. We are Slavs after all

In the last days of the war, with Patton's army within an hour's drive from Prague, Czechs rise against the Nazis in the hope that Patton would be in town by midday and they would be home for grandma's dinner. Ike orders Patton to stay put and leave Prague for the Russians, who, however, can't be bothered to turn up, leaving the Czechs to stew in the astonishingly unprecedented discomfort of four days of fighting and a looming massacre, from which they are saved by the pro-Nazi renegade Russian Vlasov Army turning against their German masters on the last day of the war. By the time official liberation arrives in Russian tanks, every Czech has been an anti-Nazi fighter, a devout socialist, and lover of Russian songs all his life.

## 14. And socialists to boot

Within three years, whoever has not been able to prove his devout socialist and Russian-song-loving pedigree at least one generation back is in jail or forced labour, thinking himself lucky to be alive. The only exception are professional gestapo helpers, whose expertise is now needed to deal with all the above, and whose pedigrees are doctored accordingly.

## 15. But human, too, maybe

Another twenty years on, the erstwhile young enthusiastic persecutors of their less enthusiastic peers turn their middle-aged unwavering enthusiasm to the futile effort of plastering a sloppily designed phantom human face on an incorrigibly inhuman system. Six months later, they are flummoxed by the puzzle of how come their persecuted peers are not welcoming and backing them when they themselves are joining the ranks of the persecuted, following the arrival of true socialism's face in Russian tanks.

## 16. Velvet-proud

A further twenty five years on, five years after communist power structures "velvetly" collapse around the Czechs, not a single communist has been brought to account for the forty years of creeping and all-pervasive misery inflicted on the nation, and the nation's most popular politicians include erstwhile active communists turned devout free-marketeers and staunch democrats. Hard-working citizens resign themselves again to second-class status as they watch shrewd communist secret service agents change into ruthless capitalist bankers, investment fund chiefs, majority stake holders, property speculators and owners of some of the country's most precious assets with the power to bribe or threaten anyone at any time for whatever reason – *forever*.

And you expect the Czechs to retain a modicum of sanity while remaining loyal – to an *idea*?

*** 

## Passing the buck

Disclaiming responsibility is another popular game, and most Czechs pass through their lives blaming just about everybody else for just about every one of their failures and disasters, personal as well as national. If they can't point their finger at anyone specific, they blame the weather, the government, the Party, international politics, and, of course, "historical events" or even "historical inevitability", of which they perceive themselves victims without choice.

It restores a bit of comfort in their uncomfortable lives. It comforts a Czech to know he has not been able to pursue a successful writer's career or complete his adult education course in the evenings because since the children were born, there has never been anywhere in the home to sit and think, let alone write. It comforts him to know that the 1946 free election voters who gave the communists 40% of the vote, and the paralysed democratic parties who did not resist the full-scale communist take-over two years later, are the ones responsible for every misery inflicted on him personally, including the fact that he has never had a good enough reason and motivation to learn English. It comforts even the staunch pro-Western Czech to understand that the nation's unfortunate post-war sympathy for the Soviet Union was, of course, the direct responsibility of the French and Brits who could no longer be trusted after their Munich betrayal.

It is fascinating to read a 1945 article by a French-educated Czech professor of Romanesque literatures commenting on the post-war re-launch of French cultural institutions in Prague, at a time when growing Soviet and communist influence was becoming very noticeable indeed.

"And they dare come back as if nothing had happened, as if they had nothing to apologise for. No – they will have to struggle hard to regain our betrayed sympathies."

Betrayed, victimised, persecuted, downtrodden, outnumbered, outgunned, outmaneuvered, left behind, misled, hoodwinked, stabbed in the back – anything would do in the place of responsibility. Taking responsibility could be too risky, too dangerous, too uncomfortable. One may even have to stand up and be counted. One may, heaven forbid, even have to fight – and get hurt.

"Nothing to do with me – I'm just a musician", is the traditional Czech response to responsibility. No wonder Czechs call themselves a "nation of musicians".

Better leave it all to "them". The all-powerful "they" are always a good excuse for my failure, poverty, poor health, incompetence, lack of drive or skill, character defects, resignation to mediocrity. Whoever "they" are. Parents, teachers, peers, capitalists, communists, the police, the Party, the anonymous apparatus, the Russians, the French, the planet, the stars – or just an abstract "they" which no one bothers to identify any more.

It's all their fault. Never mine. And survival becomes so much easier when you know that.

This Jewish joke, which comes from Czech Jewish anthologies, could not have been thought up anywhere else:

Moskovitz and Finkelstein run two groceries competing in the same street. One day, Moskovitz meets a young girl who used to come regularly to do the small family shopping, but hasn't done so for some weeks.

"Good morning, young lady, and how come you've stopped shopping with me? Are my goods not good enough? Are they too expensive?"

"No, Mr Moskovitz, but they told us in school that you people killed Jesus."

"Oh, no, Miss, not me – it was Finkelstein."

\*\*\*

# Slogans

The Czechs are suckers for a good slogan. Give them a good slogan, and they will queue up for you and teach their children diligently to do the same. Try to lead them without a slogan, and you are in for a great disappointment. Those who knew this ruled them with ease. Those who didn't had a rough time.

But what is a good slogan to a Czech?

*Truth Triumphs* is one which has survived centuries and has been used successfully by every government, and most successfully by some of the craftiest liars among Czech rulers. It is associated with St. Wenceslas, but no one is quite sure who the genius was that made it up or when. It is claimed to have been popular with Czech kings, and it was a part of the presidential regalia in the enlightened times of Masaryk, through the German occupation, and during communist rule. It became more prominent again when it was hackneyed endlessly in Havel's first presidential campaign in December 1989, in his dramatically innovative enlarged version *Truth and Love Shall Triumph over Lies and Hate.*

What is it about this slogan that can make Czechs so sentimental?

It is comforting. It soothes a Czech to know that whatever disaster he might be going through, truth will triumph. He knows that the truth is not triumphing right now, but that it will triumph eventually. Some day. It just has to. Because it does. St Wenceslas says so. Never mind what the truth is, as long as it triumphs. Never mind when it will actually triumph. Never mind how it will triumph. It will triumph by itself. On its own. No need to argue the truth out. No need to prove it. So whenever someone comes up and says that truth will triumph, this must be the time when it will. It never does. And when it doesn't, it's nobody's fault. Its time just hasn't come yet. But it is soothing to know it will.

So again: what is a good slogan to a Czech?

Modern psychology divides people into several sensory types according to the prevailing sense with which they perceive the world. Every nation, of course, has people of all types, but on a collective consciousness level, one or another sense dominates.

To persuade the predominantly *auditory* English, it all has to *sound* right.

To the *visual* German, everything must *look* neat.

The *saporous* Italians must have everything presented in good *taste*.

Whatever does not sound right to the Englishman, *stinks* to the *olfactory* American.

Czechs are mainly *kinesthetic* – and things must *feel* good to them. Above all, things must make them feel good about themselves. You must give them a slogan they can touch, feel, get emotionally involved in, wrap themselves in and feel cuddled, supported, protected.

Give their socialism a human face. Wrap their revolution in velvet. Cushion the impact of market reform. That sort of thing.

Heaven forbid your slogan should mean anything or have some logic. The more absurd and meaningless it is, the better it works. It has to bypass reason and go straight for the gut, where it can plant its seed, take root, germinate, blossom in bright colours, and become a reality that no one questions because that's just the way things are. Above all, avoid slogans which suggest they must do something, make an effort, or go somewhere. However much Czechs love and admire America, *Per ardua ad astra* would not move them one inch.

36

Unless, that is, you can persuade them that *Work Ennobles*, as did the communists when they were sending former businessmen, company managers, lawyers, teachers and journalists to coal mines or road construction. The similarity with Auschwitz's *Arbeit Macht Frei* somehow escaped everybody at the time. So much did work ennoble everyone that *Work Be Praised* became the everyday greeting which successfully replaced Good Morning in large sections of the population.

*Neither Profit, Nor Fame* was the famous slogan of the patriotic revivalist sports organisation *Sokol* (Falcon) which became the paragon of Czech righteousness in the nineteenth century and carried through to the communist takeover in 1948, after which the organisation was banned as an enemy of the working people and its leaders sent to labour camps. Very comforting slogan indeed. It never occurred to anyone that if you followed it through logically, you would end up destitute and ignored. There's nothing intrinsically wrong with being either. But the slogan made both into a national virtue. That came to its logical conclusion as the nation did indeed become destitute and ignored. And wondered how come.

*The Country's Well-being* is another effective slogan which has been played on the Czechs in a variety of ways by every regime. *The Country's Well-being Be Our Highest Law* was the slogan of the Czech fascists after Munich and the occupied Protektorat's puppet government. *The Republic Is Ours* and *We Shall Not Give The Republic Away* were two of the popular slogans in the struggle against imperialism and its agents within.

*Build Your Country and You Shall Strengthen Peace* was a particularly good patriotic internationalist work-ennobling peace-loving slogan which hung writ large on socialist construction sites and was chanted by enthusiastic masses along with *Forward Left, Not a Step Back*, as everybody was *Living Better, Living More Joyously* and marching *Towards Glittering Tomorrows*. Because, as the slogan coined by the first working-class president reminded everyone, *One Cannot Live in the Old Ways*. So they all tried to behave *progressively, comradely, working-classly, socialistly, marxistly* and *leninistly, internationalistly* but not, heaven forbid, *cosmopolitanly*.

Peace, of course, became another thing worth not only building and defending, but fighting for. *Fighting for Peace* was such an everyday natural thing to do that few people realised it was – as an unpublished poet kept reminding his friends – like "fucking for virginity".

The mighty "we", and the ever-important feeling of belonging is more fertile ground. *We Shall Remain Faithful* was the post-Munich slogan expressing loyalty to resigning President Beneš who had made the decision – against the will of the army and the people – to hand the Republic over to Hitler without a shot. *We Are With You, Be With Us* was the endlessly repeated slogan in the first week of the Soviet invasion while Dubček and Svoboda were signing a capitulation treaty.

Today, Czechs often ask themselves how such a well educated and kind-hearted nation could have fallen for such evil stupidity and keep it going for forty years. The answer is obvious. Like no one before, the communists had the Czechs stitched up with kinesthetic slogans bombarding all their senses from all sides. Left, right, and centre, morning, noon, and night.

It is now often claimed that Czechs have become allergic to slogans and cannot be fooled by them again.

Nonsense. They have only become allergic to certain type of slogans. The type of slogans which look like slogans, because they've seen them before. Forgetting that they fell for those slogans only because those slogans did not look like slogans then. They looked like what the majority of Czechs wanted to hear and feel at the time.

Make up a new slogan that catches their desires today and makes them feel good about themselves. They'll queue up for you again.

*Marching into Europe. Aiming For Greater Prosperity. Creating Cash Flows.*

And *Thinking Marketly* (oh, yes, and freemarketly at that).

\*\*\*

## The search for meaning

The Czechs have always been so puzzled by their survival as a distinct nation that they believe their existence and history must have a meaning or even purpose. Such notions may be totally incomprehensible to normal nations like the Brits, the French, or the Dutch who just get on with their national lives in the best way possible at a given time. But "national meaning" has always been a popular game east of the Rhine, where whatever one does is expected to be in some way or other subservient to an overall grand national design. Nationally meaningful, as it were.

The Germans see themselves, and themselves alone, as chosen to civilise and westernise their eastern neighbours, more efficiently than anyone else would – should anyone else ever bother – and would therefore regard anyone else's bothering as interference in their natural rightful historical purpose. The Catholic Poles are there to save Christian Europe from godless eastern barbarians, since no one else is in the position to do it. Russians believe their mission is to give the soulless world true spirituality which only their deep souls possess.

The Czechs have no idea what the hell they are here for — except, perhaps, as musicians. But since they keep surviving as a nation with recognisable distinct culture and character traits, they believe they should go on racking their brains trying to find out why continued existence keeps afflicting them.

But before they can define their national meaning, they must, of course, first define the meaning of meaning:

"Meaning is at one time the main content, at another time the main supporting force, at yet another time a cutting edge idea, at other times the main or overriding national task, national mission or programme, or even quest for glory."

Thus spoke leading Czech historians in 1928, presumably with straight faces, at a famous symposium "On the Meaning of Czech History", which was recorded for posterity and from which the Czechs have not been able to recover. And went on:

"The essential thing is the assumption that in a nation's history, one can trace a single underlying idea, a single trend, in other words a single 'meaning' as the creative element and carrying force, also assuming indirectly that all nations are carriers of 'meanings', presumably each of a different one."

No kidding. But wait:

"The term 'meaning' is usually used as an opposite to the actual material of history, the word itself expresses the requirement of interpretation of actual historical events and their contexts, particularly value judgment, a definition of an ideological value or guideline of events. But occasionally it covers more: meaning is understood to be that which is, as it were, primary or eternal in history, of which actual events are only an outward manifestation, the emphasis being on the understanding of the goal or purpose of developments, on its logical-teleological nature, and on the desire to bring down the last remaining curtain on the mystery of life."

Wonderful stuff, and all verbatim. But you have seen nothing yet:

"The search for meaning in national history is an assignment to establish what our methodologies define as interpretation of history or philosophy of history, based on facts scientifically ascertained. The issue is essentially nothing other than knowledge of the main factors of historical developments and interpretation of contexts created by them. Whoever so wishes may regard this definition of the assignment as the first step towards the actual assignment defined by the broader sense of the word 'meaning', for which, however, empirical historical science is not adequately equipped and whose very possibility it views with skepticism, although the solution to the problem in the higher sense of the word would not be possible without the first step described previously."

Having had it so clearly explained, and never wanting to appear stupid, every Czech makes sure other Czechs believe he understands clearly not only what being Czech means but even what the meaning of being Czech means, knowing that other Czechs will never dare ask him to define it lest they themselves appear ignorant.

Thus they all talk with deep understanding about various aspects of their everyday "czechness" (*českost*) or the more exalted "czechianity" (*češství*), of non-czechness, quasi-czechnes, and anti-czechness. And even a delightfully derogatory petty-czechness called *čecháčkovství* which incorporates everything every Czech hates about every other Czech and never sees in himself: cowardice, sycophancy, lack of self-esteem covered up by know-it-all and petty dictatorial habits, anxiety to make a good impression, and the cheap outsmarting and outmaneuvering skill for which they have created an ingenious linguistic gem *vyčůranost*. This wonderful word translates as the ability not just to take the piss out of someone but also to outpiss, bypiss, and overpiss.

But if you asked an educated Czech friend to give you a sincere outline of what he truly believes he and his nation are here for and what it is they have been so doggedly plodding on towards, he would probably conclude that the Czechs' national meaning is the same as their national desires and aspirations, such as these:

a) Like few nations around them, the Czechs have a deeply ingrained desire and an unwavering determination to better themselves – materially, intellectually, and culturally – whatever the circumstances, and through their own effort.

b) Unlike some other nations with similar determination, they prefer to go about it without encroaching on other nations, and even take pains to get out of other nations' way. This is so not because they would be exceptionally fair-minded, but because they sincerely regard war as a very stupid waste of time, and view everything to do with military matters with utter contempt.

c) Their aim is nothing less than being at the very top of the European league where they believe they belong and where they still vaguely recall having once been – economically, culturally, and in whatever other area of competition they may consider relevant at a given time.

d) Whenever they are left alone to get on with this determination, they go about it as methodically – if not so rigidly – as the Germans (whom, incidentally, deep down, they regard as inferior in every respect except militarily, including their military approach to business conquest, as it appears to the Czechs these days).

e) They want the world to recognise them on their own merit, not as someone else's tandem.

f) They consider themselves – not the Germans – the natural rightful business leaders of Central and Eastern Europe which they recall they have always fed, clad, shod, housed, armed, machined, and vehicled.

g) To achieve these goals, they go out of their way to inform themselves about, seek and absorb voraciously everything and anything they can learn to that aim.

h) They are fast learners and tend to remember what they learn, for as long as it is usable, and sometimes long after it has become useless.

i) While highly adaptable to changing circumstances, they turn whatever they pilfer or whatever is flogged on them into something specifically and recognisably Czech – good or bad.

j They have a unique knack for screwing up when it really matters.

Which is why they are where they are, not where they know they ought to be.

\*\*\*

## Interlude: The Other Tribe

The first thing one must know about the Moravians is that they regard the Bohemian Czechs as vastly inferior in everything other than beer-drinking. In fact, the only people whom the Moravians do not regard as inferior are the Tuscans, with whom they share a passion for and a pride in a meal well eaten and a bottle of wine well drunk.

Throughout the communist era, and against tremendous odds, through secret networks of country relatives and friends, Moravians fought like lions to preserve sporadic unofficial pockets of good living. With fine wine vintages distributed strictly among friends before they could reach state-run distribution. With culinary treats which included game and venison when Prague had to queue for pork sausages, and at least three types of fresh vegetables available throughout the year. This subversive stubbornness must surely be acknowledged as something close to a miracle by anyone who recalls the despair of having to resort to sauerkraut, sauerkraut, and sauerkraut as the only vegetables available in any form or shape in any Prague restaurant even three years after the fall of communism.

"This is old Moravia, sir," was the reply Moravian expatriates on their first return visit in the velvet revolution winter were getting from Moravian waiters proudly serving mixed salads of grated fresh carrots, white cabbage, red cabbage, kohlrabi, radicchio, and chicory, which Prague waiters would not have remembered having seen, heard, or imagined anyone would order, let alone eat.

If you speak Czech and want to be served decent wine in Prague, you would be well advised to cultivate a broad Moravian accent, just for the restaurants. This usually discourages waiters from arguing with you about the substandard wine they have served you, and makes them more likely to exchange it for a better bottle. They have to take your word for it, because they themselves can't tell the difference. And you can't blame them, they don't know any better. They have been kept in this dark ignorance deliberately by the Moravians who have always retained the best wines for themselves, leaving the poor Praguers what they themselves would not even cook a stew with, persuading them it was top quality. If your Prague waiter happens to be Moravian himself, he will not even dream of giving someone with your Moravian accent anything but the best Moravian wine he has, leaving the bad one to the Praguers.

Probably the most useful accent for this purpose would be the central Moravian regional accent of the ancient university town of Olomouc, which tends to have a strange mellowing and disarming effect on most Praguers who will soon start imitating it and have a lot of fun doing so.

Most Bohemian Czechs think of the Moravians as an appendage which has always belonged to them, and view them with amusement as a livelier and chummier wine-drinking version of their beer-drinking selves. More pastoral, less spoilt by greed and lust for power, more laid-back and fun-focused. Some Czechs even go as far as believing the Moravians to be more straightforward, reliable and honest. This, in turn, amuses the Moravians, who remember that they have bred some of the nation's finest hoodlums, including the first communist President and the last communist Prime Minister.

The Bohemians tend to forget this, and the Moravians do not remind them. What they do remind them of instead is that the four Czechs recognised even by the Bohemians as the nation's greatest achievers throughout history were all Moravians:

*Komenský* – Jan Amos, known worldwide as *Comenius*, one of Europe's late renaissance great Protestant philosophers and educators who went into Dutch exile after the defeat of Czech Protestant armies by Catholics in 1620.

*Palacký* – František, piously nicknamed "Father of the Nation", 19th century historian who re-created

Czech history as a science and was responsible almost single-handedly for restoring to Czechs their national identity and a modicum of self-respect.

*Masaryk* – Thomas Garrigue, statesman and philosopher, Czechoslovakia's first President from 1918 to 1935.

*Baťa* – Jan and Thomas, two generations of ingenious shoemakers who conquered the entire world within fifteen years of starting their business in the small Moravian town of Zlín, and lost their accent on the *t* when they moved their headquarters to Canada in 1939.

Recently added to the list of great Moravians must be:

*Kundera* – Milan, probably the most successful and best known Czech writer of all time, expatriate in France, singularly detested by domestic Czech intellectuals for reasons only they understand (or do they?).

Extended to Moravians who were German speakers, the fame list would include:

*Mendel* – Gregor, 19th century biologist, founder of genetics.

*Freud* – Sigmund, founder of psychoanalysis.

*Husserl* – Edmund, philosopher, founder of phenomenology.

*Schindler* – Oskar, saviour of 1,000 Jews from the Holocaust.

And to be fair to Moravians who found their fame in English-speaking countries, one would have to include:

*Reisz* – Karel, film director, emigrated to Britain in 1938 aged 12.

*Stoppard* – Tom, playwright, emigrated in 1939 aged 2 and arrived in Britain a few years later via Singapore and India.

*Trump* – Ivana, a model achiever.

True, there have been some achievers among the

Bohemian Czechs, but in an in-depth interview, most of those would admit to having had at least one Moravian grandparent.

N.B. Alberto Moravia was not Moravian.

The pastoral image the Czechs have of Moravia goes by the wayside once one discovers that statistically per capita, Moravia is about 25% more densely industrialised than Bohemia. Moravians just like to give the impression that they have been able to mitigate the environmental effect of industry and are living in cleaner air. This is, of course, an illusion which can be dispelled by one visit to the Ostrava region. As well as more industrialised – and thus more industrious, the Moravians believe themselves to be hardier, more persistent, more resilient, more determined, generally tougher, and sexier.

By official statistics, Moravians represent about one third of the population of the Czech Republic – approximately 3.5 million against 6.5 million Bohemians. Since most Moravians are registered in the population census as Czech by nationality (except for a few thousand jokers who registered their nationality as Moravian) – the population figures are based only on the actual population living in the two respective lands. Since half of the population of Prague is Moravian, or of Moravian parents, or of at least one Moravian parent, the true figures could be around 4.5 million against 5.5 million Bohemians.

Although Bohemian Czechs have always believed they were ruling the Moravians, the reality looks more like Moravians inconspicuously ruling the Bohemians. What makes it inconspicuous is the fact that all the ruling is done from the Bohemian capital. At the time of writing (winter 95/96), Moravians ruling the Czechs include the Prime Minister, the Chairman of the Parliament, the Minister of Economy, and the Minister for

Business Competition. One might be tempted to note as not quite accidental that between them, they have relegated the Presidency (Bohemian) to token status devoid of political power. But that could be taking the Moravian conspiracy theory too far into the realm of fantasy.

Historically, the Moravians are the older of the two tribes, and were used to statehood long before the Czechs built their first house. Their first state was organised by a Frankish merchant Samo who, while on a business trip, rallied the Slav tribes of the region in 623 for a decisive battle against the invading Avars, and was elected their king. A few years later, Samo's Moravians defeated even the Franks who tried to incorporate them into their own expanding empire. Samo left 32 sons and 15 daughters, and it is likely that subsequent Moravian rulers were recruited from this lineage.

Some Moravian-based Slav kingdoms and principalities are mentioned in Roman sources throughout the following two centuries, until the establishment of the Moravian Empire in 830 AD. This was a state of unified Slav-speaking tribes settled around the Morava river. They were christianised in 831, made literate and economically organised, and a generation later linked with the Eastern Roman Empire by two Byzantine scholars who introduced the Greco-Slav rite, one Constantine, also known as Cyril (founder of the Cyrilic alphabet) and one Method (founder of methodology — sorry, kidding, but you could be fooled there, couldn't you).

At the height of its power under king Svatopluk around 880, the Moravian Empire incorporated the whole of Bohemia and Moravia as they are today, most of Slovakia, most of Austria, the western half of Hungary, Southern Poland including Krakow, the whole of Silesia, and parts of today's eastern Germany around Meissen, Chemnitz, Bautzen, and Dresden – all of which are names of Slav origin. All those lands were then populated by Slav-speaking tribes with now extinct names like Vislani, Holasici, Glomaci, Miltians, and by Lusatian Serbs, whose dialects at the time were probably close enough to the Moravian language to give them all a sense of ethnic unity, molded by the liturgical Slavonic.

The Moravian Empire, however, did not last a whole century before it was chopped up between invading Hungarians and defending Bohemian Czechs who, having salvaged half of Moravia, incorporated whatever was left of it into their own kingdom, leaving it a semi-autonomous status, with political power shifting to Prague. Moravians settled into leaving the illusion of power to the Bohemian Czechs while trying to civilise them and make them into a bearable and presentable people. After a millennium of this frequently frustrating endeavour, some Moravians think the Czechs are now almost getting there and worth the trouble, while others still believe all their effort has been a waste of time.

# II.

# The Legends

The folk legends nations identify as their own specific lore are decisive in how a nation views itself, how it places itself among nations, how it behaves in critical moments, how it treats itself and other nations. Legends are what determines their national temperament and psychology, and what gives them a sense of tradition, antiquity, continuity, and purpose. Knowing a nation's legends might help us understand how a nation thinks in given circumstances, what its deeply ingrained codes of conduct are, and even predict how it is likely to behave in a given situation. In other words – how they have programmed themselves and their lives.

Identifying with Abraham, Isaac, Jacob, Joseph, and the grand-scale event of liberation by Moses is what keeps the Jews going against all odds in their unending quest for freedom, justice, and improvement of the human condition. The legend of King Arthur and his round table knights gave the Brits their chivalry, gallantry, sense of adventure, club loyalty, and fairness. The Niebelungen are probably what gave the Germans their sense of duty, determination, discipline, organisation skills, and drive for perfection, but possibly also the desire to make everything and everyone within reach subject to their uniformity.

The Czechs have as many legends as any other Europeans, but it is very difficult to trace an identifiable character trait or behaviour pattern from the motley of characters and events which, though identifiably Czech, do not all together give a straight-line story or a reliable insight into the Czech psychology. While it is possible to predict more or less how a Jew, a Brit, or a German would behave in certain circumstances – i.e. how his national identity would dictate to him that he should behave – the Czech can be relied upon to be unpredictable.

This is probably the first attempt to figure the Czechs out from their legends, or look at the legends with the purpose of identifying some recognisable character traits, temperament features, or behaviour codes formed by them.

*\*\**

## Czech the Forefather

This nation-founding and epoch-making story goes as follows:

Here he comes with his folk and cattle, and his brother Lech with his folk and cattle, from somewhere east of the Vistula river where he couldn't see eye to eye with other Slav tribes, and gets as far as the Central Bohemian mount of Říp which looks like a single beautiful full firm young woman's breast. There he and his folk, though tired from long voyaging, quickly and effortlessly defeat the local population who do not speak their language and settle to a bucolically uneventful life in this "promised land teaming with beast and fowl and flowing with honey, land of plenty and land well defensible against enemies", which his folk decide to name after him.

As the men tend their herds and defend them against wild beasts while others build huts and forts and the women weave and knit and make linen and canvas and sew garments, garb, attire, raiments, apparel and accoutrements, all singing pastoral songs and playing shepherds' pipes, carving gods out of wood and fearing forest fairies, the chief Czech dies peacefully thirty years after his arrival, at the age of 67. The bereaved folk place his body on a tall woodpile and wail and sing funereal songs as the wind blows the smoke away, while his brother Lech moves back north-east to establish the Polish nation. Then they collect the ashes and place them in a sepulchral mound on the mount of

Říp, which later becomes a small basilica right at the top, giving the breast mountain a beautiful erect nipple.

And that's the whole legend.

God, what a painfully boring story. What a dull, uneventful, meaningless, unexciting, passionless, undramatic way of becoming a nation.

And what does it tell us about the Czechs? Or rather, what are the Czechs trying to tell themselves about themselves here?

Well, one thing we already know: They crave, idealise, and wax lyrical about effortless, easy-going, pastoral, bucolic, gentle, homey life in comfort, tending their fat little cattle and tilling their rich little land, chasing away the bad little wolf, fearing those bogey little gods and fairies, receiving tenderness from their lovely little women and laying their heads on their lovely buxom bosoms, having a lot of good sex, playing music and telling jokes – and prospering no end, with no enemies in sight. They love everybody, and everybody loves them. That's the way they would like things to be – forever.

No drama, please, we are Czechs.

For that, of course, they would have to go to a desert island, not the heart of Europe.

The more important thing, however, is what they do not tell us in this story. What they censor out of their pastoral idyll. What they don't want to think about, be bothered by, or be reminded of.

For instance: Just how effortlessly did they defeat the local population who did not speak their language? Who were those people, for that matter? What exactly happened to them?

So let's play the account of that event back, in slower motion and in detail:

"The settlements were few and far between and their residents, speaking a foreign tongue, skin-clad, few in number though bold and brave, blocked their way and resisted them with weapons. Czech and Lech and their folk defeated them, destroying their wretched homes of shacks and hovels and holes in the ground, and moved on, forest after forest."

That is the full account of a glorious conquest. And note this:

a) The story expresses no pride in what looks like an unquestionable and unqualified military success, and it eschews the obvious opportunity to present Forefather Czech, or at least some Joshua-type warrior in his army, as a hero.

b) It passes no judgment on those wretched people, offers no ideological justification for attacking them other than plain desire for the land they occupy.

c) The way it describes the enemy suggests an inferior culture, hardly any organised economy, a neglected land waiting for the skilled hand of the cultured and civilised Czechs, as they always like to perceive themselves.

d) It gives no indication whatsoever as to whether the defeated local population was slaughtered, expelled, subjugated, or assimilated. No enslavement of men, no raping of defeated maidens is reported.

To sum up:

Forefather Czech's army surely must have had a few skilled cutthroats in its midst. Frankish sources of that time, indeed, speak of troops of rogue Slavs making sorties into the German tribes' territories with ample looting taking place, including the taking of women. But Czechs – for that is who those rogues must have been – prefer to view themselves as cultivators, civilisers, and idyll creators, rather than invaders. Memories of successful battles are played down, details censored, viewed as embarrassment, not glory.

We now know that the local population speaking a foreign tongue must have at that time (6th century A.D.) been a mixture of:

a) Remnants of a once mighty and civilised Celtic tribe of Boios or Boemi (from whom Bohemia got its name in Roman documents of the time and thereafter) who colonised and cultivated this land from the 4th century B.C.

b) Various Germanic tribes who ran it over in several waves in the great migration of nations starting around the end of the fourth century A.D., and who at this stage were probably still on the move, unsettled, not quite sure this was where they wanted to stay, and not sufficiently attached to the land to set up a well organised economy, or put up a fierce fight in its defence. Hence their makeshift homes.

The most likely outcome of the Czech invasion would have been another Westward movement of the Germanic tribes, and assimilation of the remaining Celts into the Czech population. This view would seem to be supported by the fact that Celtic words survived in ancient local names – not only of the very names of Bohemia and Moravia but of a number of towns and rivers, while German local names began to establish themselves around the 12th century with the arrival of German tradesmen, craftsmen, and farmers at the invitation of Czech kings. One region of Southern Bohemia never stopped playing the indigenous Celtic bagpipes – to an almost recognisably Irish beat.

It is fairly safe to assume that the Czechs – and probably even more so their Moravian tribe – have a strong streak of the pig-headed Irish and the melancholy Welsh still running in their veins. It may well be precisely this streak that so often drives the Czechs to a feeling of defeat and despondency. It may also be this very same streak that makes them feel so different from all the other Slavs. And it may also be precisely this streak that makes them prefer lyrical, comfortable and struggle-free inertia and innocuous comedy to the heroic, passionate, and so often tragic dramas of the Poles, the Russians, and the Southern Slavs.

The Czechs see themselves – and want to be seen – as tillers, not conquerors. Craftsmen, not warriors. Lovers, not rapists. Lyricists, not dramatists. Stand-up comics, not run-around tragedians.

\*\*\*

### Krok

And the dullness continues.

The chief of chiefs having died childless and intestate, his departure is followed by a period of lawlessness (the story makes it sound like a couple of hours and some stolen cheese) which makes the Czechs elect the righteous judge Krok as their ruler, on the advice of Lech who doesn't want to come back to govern, having by now won a few Polack wars and established the towns of Gniezdno and Krakow, and dreading the prospect of returning to the dullness of Czechdom.

Please note: there is no power struggle, no little chieftains are trying to take over, no family feuds have broken out, no one is reported to be murdered or dying in fight. Highly unlikely, of course. But since we have no other account from another source, we can't but take old Czech reporting at face value.

But let us note again: No Czech is remotely interested in fighting for and assuming the responsibility of the highest state office. Or so the Czechs like us to think.

In line with the by now well established tradition of uneventfulness, Krok "rules the Czech lands justly, judges them and teaches them wisdom, setting up schools of worship, old songs, prophecies and magic," and establishes the castle of Vyšehrad overlooking the Vltava in Prague 2 as the intended seat of future Czech rulers. Under his rule, "blessing returned to all the Czech lands, everywhere people could get on with their peaceful work, the spear and the arrow were in use only to slay beasts, people diligently cultivated the land, felling forests and establishing new fields and villages," as the Czechs love each other and multiply, undisturbed.

All that pastoral tedium is supposed to be happening at a time when Europe and the Mediterranean are teeming with events:

Emperor of Eastern Roman Empire Phocas Murdered
Northumbrians Defeat Britons at Chester
Persians Take Damascus and Jerusalem
Avars and Persians Attack Constantinople
Arabs Attack Persia
Frankish Merchant Samo Frees Slavs from Avars
Samo Builds Slav Empire
Mohammed Flees Mecca
Persians Defeated by Byzantines at Nineveh
Catholic Rite Wins Western Europe
Jews Expelled from Gaul, Burgundy and Lombardy
Mohammed Dictates the Koran
Spain Becomes a Visigoth Kingdom
Mohammed Captures Mecca
Anglo-Saxons Go Christian
Arabs Found Islam
Arabs Destroy Persian Empire
Arabs Destroy Alexandria's Books
Arabs Overrun North Africa
Plague Breaks Out in England
Venice Elects First Doge
Arabs Invade Spain

Are the Czechs not even reading the headlines? Or do they think they are living on another planet altogether?

Do the Czechs perhaps have an ostrich-like tendency to remain oblivious of events and signs around them until there's nothing they can do to influence them?

You've got it.

***

## The Princess and the Ploughman

So isn't something dramatic going to start happening to the Czechs just like to everybody else at long last?

No, it isn't.

But to make life a bit more interesting for his Czechs, Krok does leave behind him not a legislative legacy or governing rules but three lovely daughters. Of these the youngest, most beautiful, wisest, kindest, gentlest, and friendliest is elected by the Czechs as their ruler. Her name is Libuše and she becomes the first Czech worth writing an opera about, Smetana being the culprit.

She rules and rules, and people from afar come to her to sort out their problems. She does. Over and over again. And her rulings are accepted. Over and over again.

Until...

Aye, there's drama brewing.

A landowner refuses to accept her ruling that part of his land was gained unlawfully and belongs to someone else, and raises his voice thus:

"A woman! Woman of long hair but short brains! Let her knit, not rule! Shame on us! Is there another people that would allow itself to be ruled by a woman? Better to die than suffer such humiliation!" And so on.

To cut another tedious story short, Libuše concedes and sends messengers to seek out the man of her heart who would rule her dissatisfied Czech male chauvinist pigs. To establish a democratic socialist tradition in Czech politics, she has chosen a humble ploughman (not many kings available in those days), who accepts the messengers' offer to become their sovereign with these words:

"Shame you came so fast. If you had allowed me to complete this furrow, bread would be plentiful for all time in this land. But because you rushed and cut my work short, be warned that hunger will visit this land at times."

A realist, at last.

And off to the Castle he goes to take the delightful princess in his strong healthy peasant-stock embrace and sire a mighty dynasty which is to rule Central Europe throughout the Middle Ages, extending its territory at times from the Baltic to the Adriatic, having first prudently beaten ploughshares into swords.

And never again would Czechs tolerate women in politics.

***

### Women Warriors

But Czech women don't give up easily.

And this is the story of Libuše's ladies-in-waiting feeling persecuted following the Princess' death. Led by a brave beauty called Vlasta (later to become the name of a popular women's weekly), not willing to resign themselves to the status of second class citizens, they set up a castle called Děvín – ("girls' castle", literally) with a feminist military academy for girls dissatisfied with their humble status. All this to the merriment of the male population who come to watch the women's horsemanship, swordsmanship and spearsmanship games as popular entertainment – shouting abuse at them, as men often do when women engage in what men regard as their prerogative.

One day, suddenly, the women decide they've had enough, ride out in full military gear, and slaughter the hecklers to the last man.

As reports of their success spread through the land, more dissatisfied girls join the feminist ranks and set out to massacre the male oppressors, such as husbands, fathers, and elder brothers. One of the popular games was sending the most desirable girls out into the woods to woo a handsome young man into losing his guard in her arms, and then have him and all his male companions ambushed and slaughtered. (No rape is reported by any sources.)

This goes on until the ageing Prince Přemysl – who must for a while have regarded this as a God-sent opportunity for his complacent and pacifist male population to get some real war action training – realises that if he lets this training drag on for too long, he might soon have no male population left to train. So he organises a mighty army of by now no doubt very horny male peace-makers and sets out to plunder the girls castle, suppress the rebellion, and bring survivors back home to their men, to be women and wives to them once again. (Rape is not reported but strongly suspected).

The women surrender and learn to rule their men through disarming and devastating tenderness.

And what does this tell us about the Czechs?

This much:

Czech women know that feminism is not a long-term feasible strategy and consider it a waste of time.

They know better ways of getting even with men.

They don't give themselves up easily.

But when they do, they are worth the struggle.

Or did you expect something more profound?

Like what?

***

# The Flying Horse

Five generations (and five Princes' unpronounceable names) later:

Klondike bonanza.

Whose local names are an unbelievable Jílový Vrch and and an unspeakable Březový Vrch. The vowelless word "vrch" meaning hill or mountain top, we are at the dawn of the mining industry and glittering greed.

European headlines (of which the Czechs continue to be oblivious):

Charlemagne Prohibits Prostitution

Vikings Conquer Ireland

Charlemagne's Domain Extends to the Elbe River

Venice Gains Independence from Byzantium

Charlemagne Succeeded by Louis Pious

Arabs Conquer Sicily and Sardinia

Moravian Empire Founded by Prince Moimir

Danes Raid England

The most amazing of these to be oblivious to is the next door Moravian Empire, which is poised to swallow the Bohemian Czechs – to their great benefit.

People grow rich in metal but short of bread (the story tells us) as more and more greedy men abandon their fields to seek fast fortunes in the precious metal mines. Established comfortable social structures and farmers' codes of conduct begin to crumble as hungry miners start stealing food from neighbouring villages.

Village squires led by one Horymír of Neumětely visit the ruling Prince of an unpronounceable name with a petition asking for action against the miners. Petition rejected. Miners informed. Miners attack Horymír's village and pillage. Horymír flees on his wonder horse called Šemík as his village burns to ashes. Miners make merry until attacked and massacred by avenging village squires' and farmers' cavalry led by Horymír.

Survivors report to Prince. Prince sentences Horymír to death. Horymír's last wish is to have a last ride on his beloved horse inside the castle's yard.

"Up we fly, Šemík!" whispers Horymír in the horse's ear, as they approach the ramparts.

"Hold tight, master!" replies the horse.

And up they fly, like a cannonball, over the ramparts, over the hundred foot deep ditch outside, and gallop back to Neumětely, where the heroic horse dies of exhaustion and wishes to be buried outside the village gate.

Horymír is pardoned.

Vowelless words become the acid test of foreigners' ability to learn Czech.

*Strč prst skrz krk* is the ultimate giveaway.

Many Czechs find this the funniest story in their legend repertory.

As for what this could tell us about them, your guess is as good as mine.

\*\*\*

## King Barley

A generation later, the then more literate, better organised, more industrious and christianised Moravians suck the Czechs into their fast-growing empire along with the Slav-populated lands of Silesia, South Poland, Slovakia, Hungary, and Austria. Moravia's King Svatopluk, who was responsible for most of the crafty expansion, disappears without a trace and blends anonymously into the population to expiate his perceived sins and mistakes. Believing they are left kingless, the Moravians begin to look for a new king to elect, and choose a wealthy and popular but nameless squire from a castle with an unpronounceable name in the rich and fertile Central Moravian plain.

As soon as the nameless squire becomes king, he undergoes a personality crisis and turns wicked and evil like all autocratic tax-gathering monarchs. So evil is he, in fact, that his pregnant wife runs away from him to give birth to a healthy son in a barley field, whereupon the assisting farmers call the young boy Barley *(Ječmínek)*. The wife and the prince never return to the King and blend in with peasant folk.

In spite of a tireless intensive search, the King never finds his son again and becomes deeply depressed following an encounter with a pious hermit who tells him:

"Because of your sins and evil deeds, you are not worthy of your noble wife and your son. He will put right the damage you have caused. As you are the scourge of the Moravian land, so will he be its redemption. As they curse you, so they will bless him. You shall never see him. He shall appear when the Moravian land is in the gravest danger at the hand of its enemies. Only when annihilation threatens its people will Barley come with great might to salvage Moravia from a foreign yoke."

King Barley appears as a humble traveller throughout the centuries to optimistic Moravian peasants, mainly in the fields, sometimes in homes, occasionally in taverns. As long as he does not turn up with great might, Moravians know their hour of gravest danger is not here yet.

Shortly after this, Moravia is invaded by Hungarians who chop off its eastern half. Eastern Moravians disappear from history to re-emerge miraculously a thousand years later calling themselves Slovaks. The Western half is left to fight the mighty Magyars on its own for a while before being rescued and taken over by

Czechs. Whatever is left of Moravia becomes a Czech appendix forever.

King Barley becomes a popular Moravian whisky, now available matured for up to 6 years in oak casks at competitive prices.

But let us keep this in our memories for a while:

Saviour King Barley will come when Moravia is in its gravest danger.

And there are more such saviours to come.

***

### Bruncvik

The first Czech globe-trotter, reptile-hunter, and lion-tamer on record.

Following the death of his father, Prince Unpronounceable, Bruncvik (pronounced "Broontzveek", and probably a relative of Brunswick) takes over the Czech land which he rules with kindness and justice dispensed equitably to all and sundry.

By the third year of his reign this begins to bore the daylight out of him. So he sets out to travel around the world in seven years, to earn a lion for his coat of arms, to spread his country's fame, and to face challenges as a true knight. This was by now becoming the custom among bored knights, which was to culminate later in the plunder of Constantinople and Jerusalem.

Bruncvik's Odyssey reads like a sci-fi voyage through distant planets inhabited by bizarre creatures, and establishes the Czechs' flair for otherworldly fantasy and animation tricks.

Bruncvik's ship's first and last stop is Amber Mount Island, which is strewn with shipwrecks and dry bones and nothing to eat. There is no way out of here, because every time Bruncvik's ship sets sail it lands back on

BRUN
CWIK

the same island, again and again. When all his companions die of starvation, Bruncvik sees his only way out
in the claws of Legbird – a bird so big that when he
descends, darkness falls upon the island. When Legbird approaches the island next time, Bruncvik crawls
into a horse's skin, taking his sword with him. Legbird
picks the horse-clad Bruncvik as if he were a grain of
wheat, and off he flies, carrying him over the ocean for
three days and three nights, hundreds of miles away, to
distant mountains, where he drops him in his nest to
hungry Legbird chicks and flies off for more prey.
When the chicks open up the horse skin,
Bruncvik's vorpal sword goes snicker-snack, slaying
them all.

Running down the mountains far away from Leg-
birdland, Brunswick stops in a valley where, with
mighty roaring, a ferocious hydra is fighting with
a lion. Remembering that he's out there to earn himself a lion for the coat of arms, Brunswick helps the
lion defeat the hydra, only to find he has now put
himself at risk of being eaten by the lion. He runs and
runs, followed by the lion, up a tree he climbs, but the
lion sits down under the tree, waiting. After three days
and three nights of waiting, the impatient lion roars at
the tree with such might that the tree shakes and
Brunswick falls down, injures himself and can't move.
To his surprise, the lion walks away and comes back
later with a doe. They end up in each other's arms,
with Bruncvik stroking the lion's mane, never to leave
each other as long as they live.

Their joint adventures include three years of
roaming aimlessly through uninhabited lands and raft
sailing for nine days and nine nights to Carbuncle
Mount Island. This is ruled from a castle by king Olib-
rius who has two pairs of eyes, front and back. His
courtiers are a surreal motley of Star Treck extraterrestrials, some one-eyed, others one-legged, yet others

with horns, two heads, dog heads, red like foxes, half-gray half-white, some giant, others dwarfs negotiating their way between the giants' legs.

Bruncvik – the story tells us – does not feel at ease among these people and wants to leave. The king refuses to let him go until he frees his daughter kidnapped by Basilisk. This he and his faithful lion do, having first had to slay hundreds of Basilisk's hissing and spitting monsters, snakes and reptiles, and finally the fire-spitting eighteen-tail Basilisk himself.

Having returned the lovely Princess Africa (yes, Africa) to her father, he is prevented from leaving and forced to marry her. One day, sneaking through the castle's catacombs, he finds an old sword, and swaps it for his own. When told what he had found, Princess Africa rushes to lock up what she believes is still the old sword, and tells him it is a magic sword which kills when commanded by its holder: "Heads roll!".

Upon learning this, Bruncvik headrolls the entire population of Carbuncle Mount Island, loots their food and treasures, takes his lion, and sails home, doing some more headrolling on the way. He returns to his Prague castle just in time to stop his wife's wedding to another man, for seven years have passed.

Everyone welcomes and blesses Bruncvik and his faithful lion. Bruncvik rules happily for another forty years. When he dies, his faithful lion grows a double tail and moves to the Czech royal coat of arms, where he can be seen to this day. Yes, that's him alright.

Bruncvik's sword is said to be bricked up in Charles' Bridge now where the statue of Bruncvik and his lion stands, and will reappear only when the Czech lands are in their gravest danger.

Note well again: When the Czech lands are in their gravest danger, Bruncvik's sword will reappear.

If you want to know who will use it to do some more headrolling, read on.

\*\*\*

## Wenceslas

"What doeth one with a boy who as a prince was born,
   yet hath like unto a monk become?"

This is what Czech courtiers led by ruling Princess Mother Drahomira are asking themselves when 13-year old Wenceslas *(Václav* in Czech) takes the throne after the premature death of his father Prince Vratislav in A.D. 920.

For the boy, brought up by monks and his paternal grandmother Ludmila, is such a sissy that – quite out of step with princely traditions – he can read and write in Slav (liturgical Moravian), German, and Latin, knows the Bible inside out, bakes his own communion wafers, and spends more time learning religion than the art of ruling. Focusing on meditation instead of warfare. Learning kindness instead of shrewdness.

And so begins the first fully-fledged Czech homespun drama of Shakespearean proportions. With good intentions resulting in evil plots, matricides, fratricides, wars and internecine massacres, ideological conflicts, foreign intrusions, pitched emotions, complex three-dimensional characters, and falls from great heights which establish the Czech popular tradition of *defenestration* – solving political differences by throwing opponents out of windows.

The country's ideological and political background is as follows:

Having shaken off the rule of the Moravians, who had introduced the Greco-Slav Christian rite into Bohemia, the Czechs slip back into pagan worship, except for a few noble families who either continue to adhere to the Moravian church or begin to toy with the Latin rite which is now coming in via Germany.

European and Mediterranean headlines:

Plague Identified and Described by Arab Physicians

Arab Best-seller *A Thousand and One Nights* Serialised

Kabbalistic Best-seller *Sefer Yetzirah* Published

Magyars Destroy Moravian Empire

Saxon King Henry I Conquers Lorraine

And while Wenceslas goes on learning under the tutelage of monks appointed by his grandmother Ludmila, the ruling continues to be done by his mother Drahomira in the traditional fashion:

Perceiving Ludmila as the corruptor of the future ruler and a threat not only to her own power but to the safety and independence of the Czech realm, Drahomira proceeds first to have Ludmila murdered by two gentlemen with foreign sounding names, Tunna and Gomon, then to have both these murderers murdered together with all their relatives including women and children. Thereafter, she bans all monks from the presence of her son who, however, goes on meeting them clandestinely, thus learning the art of conspiracy.

In a brilliant coup d'état which legends would like us believe was bloodless (remember that Czechs have a flair for self-censorship), Wenceslas' "Righteous Party", though very much a minority in the land, defeats Drahomira's "Ignoble Party" two years later. Drahomira and her supporters are exiled from Bohemia, internecine hatred pacified (bloodlessly again, of course), and Christ's tabernacle of peace spreads over Czech lands. So begins the rule of Wenceslas the Saint, Christ's soldier who, in the service of his

Lord, causes untold damage to the devil, the legends tell us.

"Exercising Christian love and mercy and generosity to the poor, orphans and widows, priests, guests and travellers. Truthful in speech, fair in judgment, faithful to all which is entrusted to him, exceeding human limits in goodness. Never depriving anyone of anything through violence or trickery. Believing in God with all his heart, embodying goodness in all his life. Building churches in all castles and gathering God's servants from abroad, introducing God's worship as is customary in great nations. Spreading Christ's message through good example, not by force." Says one legend.

"Mortifying his flesh by rough cloth under his princely robes, suppressing his physical desires by denying himself sleep and food and abstaining from drink and lowly entertainment, striving for chastity in marriage which he accepted only as a ruler's duty to sire a son, while devoting all his life to the service of God." Says another legend.

A romantic weakling who is about to squander the family's assets, and a pious unpractical cloud-cuckoo-land religious fundamentalist lunatic unfit to unite, let alone govern, a country which is about to be sandwiched between two growing military powers – the Germans and the Magyars.

This is how Wenceslas must appear to his Czech opposition, which is joined by his equally Christian but more down-to-earth, action-focused, and possibly less internationalist younger brother Boleslav.

And there is something else the opposition could not fail to notice but which the legends omit, edit, censor. (By God, do Czechs love their self-censorship!)

At around the same time in the year 922, as Wenceslas carries out his miraculous coup, Czech lands –

history tells us unmistakably – are visited by large numbers of well-armed and well-organised troops belonging to Duke Arnulf of Bavaria, whom Wenceslas knew from his religious studies in Regensburg. There are also reports of armed visits by Wenceslas' friend Saxon King Henry I, who is now bidding for rule over the entire German Empire, including some newly conquered territories.

Not exactly a foreign invasion, and certainly not a full-scale war either, just some sinister troop movements, apparently. Just enough – one can imagine – to assist the otherwise powerless boy with no significant domestic support to grab power and start turning the bellicose and unruly Czechs into a doveish people dedicated to Christ's love and devotion to peace at all cost. Doveish enough to be drawn tighter, without undue resistance, into the grander design of a growing empire of the Germans using the convenient banner of the Holy Roman Church – or, if you want to look at it catholically rather than germanly – the Holy Roman Empire using the convenient national drive of the Germans.

Abroad, Wenceslas is rapidly gaining the reputation of an enlightened ruler who invites learned men from German speaking lands and welcomes them with gifts of gold and silver, precious garments and slaves, gives them licence to teach, preach, set up monasteries and parishes, and acquire wealth by selling religious relics including putative remnants of saints' bodies – a commodity which is gaining popularity throughout christianised Europe. This – plus a hefty annual tax he agrees to pay the German Empire – elevates the provincial Principality of Bohemia to a nation on a par with other Western nations, or so historians believe.

To domestic opposition, however, Wenceslas' rule appears more and more sinister and dangerous to the country's future and needs of the times, as can be seen from a note Czech nobles write to Boleslav.

"Prince Wenceslas leads a life that befits more a monk than a king. He believes, as if struck by a mental illness, more in life hereafter than herewith. Instead of us, the nation's nobles, he invites to his table strangers and people of no consequence. We demand that you take power sooner than later, before all your father's treasures are foolishly squandered."

The growing influence of German speakers in Wenceslas' court and the country – however economically or culturally beneficial some of it must undoubtedly be – irritates the local nobles particularly badly at a time when Saxon King Henry invades, brutally suppresses, subdues, and swiftly germanises the Slav-populated lands of Brandenburg and the Elbe river, just across Bohemia's northern border.

The time has come for faithful Czechs to strike back, even brother Boleslav now believes. He invites Wenceslas to his castle and has him neatly murdered on Monday 28th September 929 – at his church's locked door, as the legend tells us, to give Wenceslas' death a religious significance. Czech nobles swiftly follow this up with a Prague massacre of Wenceslas' supporters and their families and expulsion of foreign clergy, throwing many a man, woman and child out of the window, over the ramparts, or into the river.

Sensing a power vacuum in Bohemia and a unique opportunity to conquer and subdue yet another Slav land, King Henry promptly stages a full-scale invasion, ostensibly to avenge his beloved friend.

Bad miscalculation. For even after nine years of pacification, the Czechs still enjoy a good fight. Boleslav raises a mighty defence army and keeps King Henry and later his son Ota I busy in border battlefields for fourteen years. At the end of this, he, too, accepts confederation and agrees to pay a peace tax to the Empire. But he earns himself the enemy's respect and secures for his country equal status among all confederate lands of the Empire. And he obtains for his Premyslid dynasty (remember the Ploughman?) the Empire's backing to rule the whole of Bohemia unchallenged by other Czech dynasties, and to conquer, civilise, and incorporate into the Czech kingdom and thus into Christendom any Slav-populated lands east of the Elbe. This his descendants set out to do with glee, fire and sword – and a lot of Czech music, including the Celtic bagpipes.

The drama ends as happily as it could do under the circumstances, and thumbs up to the Czechs, you might think.

But not the Czechs.

As soon as Wenceslas is canonised by the Church, the fratricidal Boleslav is turned into the devil of devils in folk legends. In some obscure twist of popular fantasy, not Boleslav the fighter but Wenceslas the pacifier is elevated to the role of Patron of the Nation, Defender of the Czechs, who "shall not let us and future generations perish", who will take up Bruncvik's sword when Czechs are in their gravest danger and chase foreigners out of the land.

This Wenceslas legend comes from the nineteen fifties:

St Wenceslas' skeleton, which lies in his tomb, is being questioned as authentic and tested by Czech scientists who cannot come to a satisfactory conclusion. It is therefore sent for more sophisticated examination to the Moscow Academy of Sciences.

A couple of months later, a Russian academic arrives in Prague, opens his trunk, and out pours a heap of broken bones and a split skull.

"Comrades, it is your King Wenceslas, definitely."
"How did you find out?" ask the stunned Czechs.
"The bastard confessed."

Wenceslas may have been a saint, a scholar, great educator, civiliser, and maybe even a righteous ruler. But defender of his people, with sword and on horseback at the head of an avenging army? Who do the Czechs think they are kidding?

But glorification of this pacifist statesman and self-delusion about his historical role cuts so deep into Czech culture and the Czech psyche that Czech historians of the 20th century (in free Czechoslovakia, not under foreign domination) could write this, and not as a joke:

"Prince Wenceslas proved his extraordinary political talent by surrendering to the German Empire, by preferring humiliation over war, in order to secure peaceful development of his country, by agreeing to pay tax and accept political dependence, thus becoming the founder of a good tradition of Czech foreign policy".

A good tradition indeed, adhered to time and time again. Beneš in 1938. Beneš again in 1948. Dubček and Svoboda in 1968. A good tradition of betting on the wrong horse every time they are in grave danger.

As long as they go on believing, however subconsciously, that Wenceslas is the one who will take up the sword in their defence, as long as they put their destiny into the hands of statesmen steeped in his tradition, the Czechs may be great musicians – but they will remain anybody's sitting duck.

\*\*\*

### Knights of Blanik

This is St. Wenceslas' future army. Knights in full armour, with horses, living in deep caves inside the

PRAG

XII· DOMVS
SAECVLVM REGIA

Blanik mountain – in an extraterrestrial time warp. They may indeed be extraterrestrials, for nothing is known about them. Where they come from, how they got there, how long they have been there, how many there are, what they eat, what makes them tick.

Occasionally, someone strays in. One day a village girl finds herself in their cave and sweeps their floor – and probably other things as well. When she gets back to her village a couple of hours later, she is told she had been away for a year. A blacksmith is called in to shoe their horses. When he comes back home in the evening, he had been gone for a year.

But St. Wenceslas' knights are sleeping. The time has not yet come for them to get up. That time will be when Czech lands are – guess what – in their gravest danger. When so many foreigners invade it that Czechs have nowhere to hide.

Only then will all the signs be there to see: Trees in the Blanik Forest will dry up and leaves will fall. The old dry oak at the top of the mountain will go green again. Water will gush out from the tiny source and pour down into the valley. Then a mighty battle will break out by the mountainside. The lake will go red with blood. There will be weeping and great sadness, but Czechs will defend themselves valiantly against odds.

At a crucial moment, Blanik mountain will open up and knights in full armour will ride out, led by St. Wenceslas on a white horse, to help the Czechs.

The enemies, overwhelmed by sudden fear and confusion, will run away towards Prague where they will be finished off. Rivers of blood will run down the streets of Prague towards Charles' Bridge. Then St. Wenceslas on his white horse, with his banner, will lead the Czechs and chase foreigners and enemies of the nation out of the country. On that day, holy peace will be restored and the Czech lands will breathe a sigh of relief.

In the meantime, Czechs can be walked on again and again until they have nowhere to hide. Twice in a generation in one century alone.

But they can always rest assured they have never really been in the gravest danger. Grave enough, but not the gravest. For if they were, St. Wenceslas would come, wouldn't he? With his Blanik Knights, and Bruncvik's sword, right?

And King Barley – of course – good old Moravian King Barley with them.

What exactly do they expect?
Is the gravest danger yet to come?
Forever yet to come?

\*\*\*

## Magician Rye

If you can have a king called Barley, a magician called Rye (*Žito*) should come as no surprise.

Magician Rye appears on the scene in the reign of King Wenceslas IV (end of the 14th century) when, the legend claims, "anyone could walk or ride anywhere, day or night, with a nugget of gold on his head, and no one would stop him". This could mean a number of things:

a) Bohemia was a land of law-abiding citizens.

b) Bohemia's citizens were all so wealthy that a nugget of gold on someone's head would be taken as natural.

c) Bohemians were so tolerant and used to all types of eccentrics that no one gave a damn what others wore on their heads.

Every now and again, the King himself would dress up in proletarian clothes and come to the market to do his shopping. If he found a merchant cheating on quantity or price, he would reveal his identity, confiscate the merchant's goods, and have them distributed to the poor in town or to needy pupils in schools. The merchant would be punished by being put in a basket on a rope and dipped in the river.

Oh, yes, socialist justice has very deep roots in Bohemia, and is very deeply felt by Czechs, from the lowliest to the most extolled.

Wenceslas IV (the sixth *Václav* on the Czech throne, fourth as king) was a chummy fellow and enjoyed hearty entertainment bordering on popular fun. Were he in the castle today, he would prefer The Rolling Stones to Beethoven's Fifth, and Frank Zappa to Don Giovanni. Entertainment of the most popular kind was arranged for him by his court magician Rye, whose skills included:

Freezing people to the ground. Changing his appearance, including his height and face on the spot, frequently in the middle of a single speech. Turning the court jester's hand into a horn, and then into a horse-foot, and finally a calf-trotter, just as the jester was trying to grab something good to eat. None of this highbrow arty stuff. Good solid culture, know wha' a' mean?

Among the populace, he was known not only as a great entertainer but also a dangerous trickster who could cheat people out of their money by performing magic like:

Turning 30 wheat-sheaves into fat pigs and selling them to a rich and mean merchant, in whose care they turn back into sheaves. When the merchant comes to take revenge, Rye lets the merchant break his leg off, and then allows the crowds to force the merchant to make compensation for grievous bodily harm.

One day, the court is visited by the Duke of Bavaria who brings with him a troupe of entertaining magicians. So good are they and so many wonderful tricks can they perform that not only the citizens of Prague but even the King himself feels put to national shame.

It is from a deep cultural humiliation that Rye now has to salvage his nation single-handedly.

He does so by coming onto the stage where the Germans are at the height of their tricks, opens his mouth until it is bigger than himself, swallows a German performer, belches, and spits him into a barrel of water, alive.

Absolute showstopper. Everyone's eyes focus on Rye, a standing ovation follows, the King himself praises him in public, Germans crawl off the stage.

Magician Rye's most celebrated achievement.

This is all the Czechs need to feel superior to the Germans. Taking the micky out of them, and winning ice-hockey games.

***

## The Golem of Prague

After extraterrestrials, some solid science fiction – from the times of Emperor Rudolf II, height of Central European Renaissance at the end of the 16th century, in a Prague teeming with magicians, alchemists, astronomers, astrologers, and kabbalists. The Golem of Prague, as legends depict him, is a human-size computer robot, operated by a software diskette (or marble, according to some versions) called *Shem* (meaning "name" in Hebrew), controllable only by the person who places the *Shem* into a slot in its forehead – i.e. someone who knows how to operate the software.

The robot's qualities are described by allegedly contemporary rabbinical manuscripts roughly as follows:

Although looking like a human being, the Golem has no judgment of his own. Carries out all orders mechanically. Within an orbit of ten cubits (5.5 metres), he has ultimate physical power and no one can stop him. He has a higher intelligence than animals. Immune to the sword, fire, or drowning. No speech ability but, surprisingly, can give full reports of events in writing. No ability to reproduce and no sexual desire, no lusts. Not prone to any illness. Aware of time of day without the aid of clocks.

The robot – or artificial human-looking being called *golem* in Hebrew and *homunculus* in Latin – was created, formed and made by Prague's greatest philosopher of all time, Chief Rabbi, talmudist and kabbalist, Yehudah Loewy ben Betzalel, also known under the acronym Maharal, whose longevity spans almost an entire century, from 1512 to 1609. Most versions of the legend, including alleged contemporary rabbinical sources, claim that the Maharal and two assisting rabbis made the Golem in a nearby forest out of clay, using life-giving mystical tricks which no one has since been able to repeat or even identify.

The rabbinical record, allegedly written by one of the assisting rabbis, tells how the Maharal taught both assistants to recite Divine Names in different arrangements as they walked around the clay figure seven times, radiating their own life energies of fire, water, and air respectively, into the Golem, to blend with his energy of earth.

Well, maybe. It is now known, or assumed with fair certainty, that Prague alchemists of the same period knew the nuclear fission chain – or how to break the atom all the way to a nuclear explosion. Having discovered it, they destroyed all evidence and all documentation which might lead to its being repeated and misused, and garbled it up into complex lead-into-gold formulas. The same is likely about the Maharal's human-shaped computer, and the hocus-pocus clay magic story is a convenient red herring.

Someone somewhere dug out (or possibly made up) that Queen Elizabeth's chief of spies John Dee, code-named 007 (this is true) and himself an accomplished

alchemist credited with some conclusive time-travel research, listed the Golem among his prime targets to be researched and developed for England's military purposes, along with whatever useful tricks he and his lieutenant Edward Kelly could pick from Prague alchemists while on their espionage assignment there at the time.

The Golem, known to Prague Jews as Yossele the mute, was made for the single purpose of protecting the Jews from anti-Semitic riots of a local populace occasionally enraged by blood-libel stories spread by local Dominican monks and a particularly unappetising priest called Thaddeus, a converted ex-Jew turned one of the greatest Jew-haters of his time.

The blood libel, which had been banned as ludicrous by the Emperor and the Cardinal, went as follows – and this is a quote from a confession made by an apostate Jewish girl, under tuition from Father Thaddeus, on her entry into the Catholic faith, and in a court of law under oath:

"Several days before Passover, a couple of Rabbi's aides came to our home with a couple of bottles of blood. They told my father that the Rabbi had sent them to deliver blood for the holiday. My father then paid them well, and the blood was then mixed with the flour used to bake unleavened bread. I couldn't take these nauseating practices any more and decided to become a Christian."

The blood was supposed to be that of a missing maid who had run away, alleged by Thaddeus to have been ritually slaughtered, later to be found alive and well by – you guessed it – Yossele Golem on Maharal's investigation – and brought to the court just in time, before the death sentence could be imposed on a couple of accused Jews, followed, as was customary, by a pogrom and looting of the Jewish quarter.

On another occasion, Golem is reported to have caught and brought to justice a butcher who dug up a newly buried girl, brought her to the slaughterhouse, cut her up and smeared her with pig blood, and tried to plant her as evidence in the Jewish quarter.

Various versions of the legends – Jewish and Gentile – come up with all sorts of Golem-our-Hero stories, even of his misuse for dubious purposes by unauthorised people who somehow got hold of the *Shem* software. But the Golem was programmed for defence, not aggression. Patrolling the streets of the Jewish quarter at night. When there was no danger to defend against he would be left sleeping in the Maharal's home.

When attacks on the Jewish quarter cease as Prague burgers accept blood libel to be total nonsense, The Maharal and his two assistants unmake the Golem in the same way they made him. They take him to the attic of the Altneu Synagogue, and through the same kabbalistic process, take away the energies they gave him. The Golem turns into clay and disintegrates.

Among the more amusing non-Jewish latter-day Golem legends are of Prague alchemists trying to create an artificial woman – *homuncula* – who could mate with the Golem, an opportunity which English spy alchemist Edward Kelly uses to plant a woman spy in the Emperor's bed.

And of, course, the 1950's comedy film ending with the Golem joining a working class velvet revolution, giving his powers to the service of socialism, and all together singing what became an unforgettable hit of the 50s:

When all of us together
love the world and peace,
then all of us together
will work for the world at ease,
when all of us give all to all,
then all of it belongs to all.

Boy, did the communists know how to use a good story to stitch the Czechs up with more slogans.

The Golem is a legend that every Czech child grows up with and identifies as part of Czech culture and tradition. Prague has built monuments to both the Golem and his creator. It is surprising that the Golem has not joined the ranks of Wenceslas' army who will be liberating the Czechs one day when they are in the gravest of dangers.

This adoption makes Czechs one of the few Gentile nations sincerely proud of their Jewish heritage.

And good for business it is, too.

\*\*\*

## Interlude: The Oldest Tribe

Czechs are one of the nations for whom Jews feel a special affection, or whom – to use a traditional Jewish saying – they have inscribed in the Book of Life. True, they did not save their Jews from the Holocaust like the Danes (100%), the Bulgarians (100%), or the Italians (90%). The Nazi camps destroyed over 80% of Czech Jewry. But there is no Jewish record of any Czechs actively participating in the destruction – and Jews do have a keen and long memory.

Although their puppet government collaborated with the occupying Germans and implemented all the anti-Jewish measures of the Nuerenberg laws, the Czechs did not go beyond what was demanded of them on this score under the threat of their own death. Czech police, with armed German soldiers behind them, did assist the Germans in making Jewish transports from Czech cities run smoothly and orderly, but there is no record of any Czech policemen physically abusing or even insulting the people they were helping to load into cattle trucks. Nor is there any record of a Czech volunteer actively participating in running the death camps. (The Czechs did, in fact, run their own little hard labour work-to-death camp for Romanies en route to Nazi camps, as has only recently been publicly admitted).

All this may not sound like much of an achievement in kindness, until we take into account that every nation around them participated actively and with glee.

Whatever the Czechs may have failed to do to lift themselves to the class of the Danes, the Bulgarians, and the Italians, they made up for amply with a massive airlift of arms which saved the newly founded State of Israel from destruction at its birth in 1948. Israel owes its existence to Czech arms, every Israeli will quote from his history lessons.

Few Czechs failed to rejoice in Israel's victory in 1967. That, followed by the communist government's decision to break off diplomatic relations, was one of the crucial elements in the psychological fabric that gave Czech intellectuals and students the courage to stand up in the autumn of the same year and demand dramatic reforms which became known as The Prague Spring.

Czechs are generally remembered as a people among whom the Jews felt safe and at ease, in whose culture they participated fully, where no serious anti-Semitic acts beyond the odd anti-semitic joke have occurred since the mid-19th century, and where in the 1890s Professor and MP Thomas Masaryk (later to become Czechoslovakia's first President) took up and won the defence of a poor and illiterate Jew in a provincial town accused of murder on charges stupidly similar to the old medieval blood libel.

"Anti-semitism is our own scourge, and ours alone, it damages us, it demeans us, it makes us vulgar," wrote Masaryk in one of his many essays.

Israel has a Masaryk kibbutz, Tel-Aviv has a Masaryk Square. Just to check that Israelis really know who they name their squares after, I once asked a tetragenerian gentleman in Tel-Aviv's Masaryk Square who Masaryk was. His reply: "You don't know who Masaryk was? You should be ashamed of yourself."

In Masaryk's Czechoslovakia, the only country in Central Europe with no Jewish quotas imposed on higher education at the time, Jews – who formed 2.5 percent of the population – accounted for 18 percent of all university and technical college students.

Masaryk's government had four Jewish ministers half a century before British Jewry considered the same number in Margaret Thatcher's government an unprecedented emancipation.

It was, I think, Churchill who said that a nation's civilisation level is best judged by the way it treats its minorities. On this score, the Czechs may have something to feel superior about.

Jews have been present in the Czech lands probably since the second century A.D., at trading outposts of the Roman Empire, and no doubt throughout the centuries up to the establishment of the Moravian and the Czech states.

There are ample indications that the famous Frankish merchant Samo who became king of Moravian tribes in the 7th century and "preferred oriental customs over local ones" was a Jew. A smart well-travelled Frank with "oriental" customs? Well, yes, actually, why not. Later Merovingian and Carolingian court suppliers were mostly Jewish, too. Samo's name really does sound more Hebrew than Frankish. And since he left behind – how many sons and daughters? – Moravians may have 0.0018 percent Jewish blood running through their veins, and can claim their Jewish heritage all the way back to the seventh century. One up for the Czechs again.

Active Jewish participation in local business is first recorded in a customs rulebook of 903 A.D. They are spoken of mainly as itinerant merchants trading in spices, jewels, wine, textile, guns, salt, wax, skins, cereals, cattle, horses, and slaves.

Prague Jewish merchants are mentioned in the first travel report of Bohemia, written around 965 by an Arab-writing Spanish Jew, Ibrahim ibn Yakub. The Prague Jewish settlement, as described by him, lay next to the ducal market at the foot of the castle. Half a century later, there are records of Jewish quarters being established in the two major Moravian towns of Olomouc and Brno, from scattered Jewish households deciding, or more likely being ordered, to move into one part of town exclusively.

Prague's Jewish quarter, situated between The Old Town Square and the Vltava river, started as a Jewish village in mid-12th century, alongside settlements built by other foreign merchants.

The first Czech Jewish doctor we know of was one Jacob Apella in the court of Vladislav I around 1120. Some Jewish accountants and lawyers are also mentioned in contemporary records, under various titles of financial advisers and court clerks. Movie producers and press barons came much later. But Vladislav's court vizier (or whatever the title was, probably a lawyer, too) known as Podiva the Jew built himself what must have been the first Jewish castle since the destruction of Massada. It was in South East Moravia, named Podivin, with a village later established around it, growing gradually into a small town, with a Jewish community which at its height in mid-19th century numbered 648 souls representing 31% of the town's population. Some of their houses are still there.

Disaster strikes – like everywhere else in Europe – with the 1215 Fourth Lateran Council decree banning Jews from land ownership, agriculture and crafts, forcing them into buying and selling, and money-lending, turning them into despised bankers.

This is followed by several centuries of the usual fortunes and disasters alternating like a yo-yo. Following a few decades of sporadic anti-Jewish violence, special privileges are granted to Czech Jews in 1254 by King Premysl Otakar II. These make them King's subjects, guaranteeing them protection and granting licence to lend money on interest. King's privileges outlaw any violence against Jews and their property, condemn blood libel as a false charge, ban enforced baptism, disturbance of Jewish holidays and desecration of cemeteries and synagogues. Damage inflicted on Jews is treated as damage caused to King's property. Disputes between Jews and Christians are to be judged exclusively by royal courts.

While this decree remains in force on paper, succeeding kings play all sorts of jokes around it. Wenceslas II has all Jews rounded up and arrested in 1296 as part of a special "protection scheme", and releases them only upon a huge ransom payment. John of Luxemburg (1310-46) loots the Prague ghetto several times and "requisitions" substantial wealth, to be able to "finance their protection", which includes battles expanding his kingdom to re-take Silesia, parts of Poland and Austria – where, to be fair to him, Jews were worse off than under his rule. Most other kings, even those who stuck to their protection promise, use Jewish money and write off Jewish claims to pay their own debts.

During the glorious days of Charles IV, Jewish contribution plays an important part in the establishment of the university in 1348 which has its firsts lecture halls rented in the house of a Jew named Lazarus, on the outskirts of the Jewish town.

O ROTA
FOR-
TUNAE
ROTA
MOBI-
LIS

OTA
KAR
II·

REX·BOHEMIÆ

"Desecration of the host" (of the communion wafer, that is) and "causing the plague" are the main popular charges leading to extensive pogroms in Germany in the 14th century, which occasionally spill into Bohemia. The worst of these breaks out at Easter 1389 during the rule of Wenceslas IV when priest-incited mobs storm the Prague ghetto and massacre over 3,000 men, women, and children. A lament for the dead, written by one of the survivors, Rabbi Avigdor Kara, remains a part of the liturgy of Prague's Alt-Neu Synagogue. The synagogue, incidentally, is not "old-new", as its German name might suggest, but "provisional" or "conditional" – which is what its original Hebrew name *Al-tnai* meant to convey.

Little wonder that after so much pillage and massacre, the Jews welcome the arrival of the Protestant Hussites on the political scene and the battlefield. A couple of decades of mutual sympathy between Christian and Jew follow, with even some theological and philosophical interchange. The Hussite revolution allows Jews to take up crafts again, Hussite theologians argue for their emancipation, and Jews help them defend Prague and finance their armament. The Hussites draw inspiration from Jewish messianism and Jewish history, even to the point of giving their towns and fortresses names like Tábor, Sion, or Oreb.

Defeat of the Hussites leads to large scale expulsions of Jews from towns, which becomes a favoured game played on and off, whenever towns or local nobles so decide, till 1567 when Emperor Maxmilian II re-establishes all their earlier rights and comes to have himself blessed by the Prague Rabbi.

But it is under his successor, the mystical artist Rudolf II, that Czech Jewry experiences a glorious 35 years of its most creative time in its history to date. It becomes one of the three largest and most respected Jewish communities, along with Amsterdam and Salonica, and produces some of the greatest scholars of its time, of whom Yehuda Loew ben Betzalel is the most notable. That along with bankers like Mordechai Maisel who was Rudolf's "court Jew" and financial adviser, and even brewers like Pinkas.

The price to pay for this seems worth paying, but it is to alienate Jews from the Czechs for three centuries to come: In exchange for royal protection, Prague Jews have to commit themselves to making German their everyday language and take on German surnames. Until then, most of them, as recently proved by Roman Jacobson from medieval Hebrew manuscripts from Bohemia, were Czech speakers. Habsburg germanisation of the Czech lands is beginning to bite, and Jews – except for Jewish country folk who carry on speaking Czech and retain Czech names – unwittingly help move it along.

It isn't until the mid-19th century, by which time Bohemia and Moravia have 347 active Jewish communities, that Czech Jews, given full civic rights, begin to re-assert their "czechness" and join in the Czech cultural and political revival. But as late as the 1930s, some of Czechoslovakia's best Jewish writers are still writing in German.

It is to the Czechs' credit that the linguistic and cultural "germannes" of large sections of Czech Jewry did not serve them as a pretext for anti-Semitic outbursts. Not even for a "germanisers, getting what they asked for" attitude when Czechoslovakia's Jewry was being decimated.

But that's where the glorious history of Czech Jewry really ends. Out of the 120,000 Czech and Moravian Jews, 24,000 survived the Holocaust. Half of those emigrated by 1948. Half of those again in 1968. Not more than 5,000 remain now, with 4,000 in Prague.

Many of them are half-Jews, quarter Jews, or converts – including their Chief Rabbi. They are trying hard to revive Jewish communal life, but a lot of their work focuses on the precious relics of their past – for the millions of tourists who come to Prague and crowd the Jewish Town.

Czech Jews have become a museum community.

The Czechs really do love them and really are proud of them.

It really is good for business.

\*\*\*

# III.

# Events which made them

This includes events which nearly unmade them. Czechs frequently disagree between themselves on what is good and what is bad for them. There have always been even those who regarded major national disasters as the most blessed events in Czech history, in which the wiser Czechs with deeper insight, broader horizon, and longer perspective accepted or even helped bring about the rule of a higher, greater, grander, richer, more enlightened, more just, more universal, more progressive, spiritually superior, or just better armed civilisation.

Before going into a full chronological account of major events, a few words about that uniquely Czech way of solving political differences – *defenestration*.

There are three main ones, each of which had a major impact on the course of events.

### Prague Defenestration 1419

Triggers off the full blast of the Hussite revolution. In July of that year, King Wenceslas IV, under pressure from German princes and the Church, appoints anti-Hussite councillors to Prague City Hall, who introduce tough anti-Hussite measures. Prague folk led by Hussite preacher Jan Želivský storm the City Hall, throw the councillors out of the window to a furious crowd which finishes them off, convene a new council and elect new councillors and military governors. The King is forced to confirm the election and leave the defenestration unpunished. While the King is dying, Prague folk attack monasteries and kick Catholic clergy out. Prague Hussites take the Vyšehrad castle in Prague. Country Hussites come to Prague's aid, blasting every Catholic army unit on the way. The Hussites, now kingless and expecting large-scale trouble from outside, mobilise all Protestant towns, villages, and aristocracy, who start taking over and fortifying one Czech town after another. Eight months after the defenestration, the Pope declares Bohemia a heretic country and orders a crusade, led by Wenceslas' younger brother Sigmund, King of Hungary. Crusade after crusade is beaten off by the Hussites for 15 years before the nation gets exhausted and gives in in 1434.

## Prague Defenestration 1618

Triggers off the Thirty Year War. Ferdinand Habsburg, crowned King of Bohemia in 1617, reneges on every treaty that previous kings had made in respect to tolerance of the Protestant religion, and on lawful privileges the Czech kingdom was to retain within the Czech-Austrian-Hungarian confederation set up in 1526. Following a clandestine meeting in Prague in May 1618, Czech nobles march to the Castle "to have a word" with the regents Martinic and Slavata, and their chief clerk Fabricius. Following an unsatisfactory discussion, the nobles throw all three of them out of the window. Landing on a dung heap, they escaped unharmed. But the Czech nobles make their message clear. An open anti-Habsburg rebellion by Czech aristocracy follows suit, electing a government of 30 governors from the three estates – the high aristocracy, the landed gentry, and the burghers. The rebellion is crushed two years later, and an all-European war between Catholic Habsburgs (Austria and Spain), and Protestant countries breaks out.

## Prague Defenstration 1948

This does not trigger off anything, only confirms to all and sundry that an iron curtain, and darkness, has fallen on the Czechs again. Son of Czechoslovakia's first president, post-war Foreign Minister Jan Masaryk, stays in the Communist-led government which took power in February 1948, a few months before scheduled elections, in which polls were predicting a defeat for the Communist Party. Jan Masaryk was always known as a joker, but his words to the nation following the coup ring to Czech ears too much like gallows humour: "With this government, I shall enjoy governing." A few days later, he is found dead on the pavement under the window of his apartment in the Ministry. Suicide claimed. Murder suspected. Neither ever conclusively proved. Or disproved.

And now the chronology of major events.

***

## Arrival of Czechs

Probably in the course of the 6th century, settling in Central Bohemia around a sexy mountain.

***

## Samo's Kingdom

Frankish Jewish merchant uniting Slav tribes in Moravia against the Avar invasion. Kingdom lasted for 35 years, 623-658, and disintegrated after his death as his 35 sons probably portioned it out between themselves.

***

## The Premyslid Dynasty

Established around the time of Samo, centering on the castle of Vysehrad, overlooking the Vltava river, by a beautiful Princess and a virile ploughman, and lasting 6 centuries.

\*\*\*

## Great Moravia

Founded by Moimir in 830. Christianised by German missionaries in 831. The main Christian missionary work, however, is done by two religious scholars from Salonica, Constantin (also known as Cyril) and Method who arrive with a Slav Christian rite, a Slav language liturgy, Slav language translations of some Bible passages, and a Papal blessing to use it as a third permitted liturgy alongside Greek and Latin. United under a new banner, Moravia successfully defends itself against Frankish invasions and extends its borders westward to incorporate Bohemia, following its incorporation of Slovakia and parts of the then Slav-populated Hungary and Austria. Bohemia's ruler Bořivoj I of the Premyslid dynasty swears allegiance to Moravia's king Svatopluk and comes to Moravia to be baptised in the Slav rite. East Frankish king Arnulf recognises Svatopluk as the sovereign ruler over Bohemia's tribes in 890, only to re-establish his own sovereignty there five years later when the Premyslid dynasty led by one Spytihněv swear loyalty to him. Most of Bohemia switches over from Slav to Latin rite. Hungarian invasions begin to slice off Slovakia in 905. Moravian kingdom collapses under Hungarian onslaught in 907, and Moravian folk music begins to resemble the *csardás*.

\*\*\*

# Sovereign Bohemia

Vratislav of the Premyslid dynasty defends Bohemia from Hungarian invasions and unites Bohemian tribes around 920 before he dies in 921, succeeded by teenage Wenceslas, for whom his mother Drahomira rules for three years before Wenceslas takes the throne backed by German king Henry I and Bavarian prince Arnulf, whose invading armies come all the way to Prague. Bohemia's sovereignty is subjected to German patronage and taxation.

***

# Wenceslas and Boleslav

Wenceslas' German-backed rule comes to a dramatic end when he is murdered by his younger brother Boleslav in 929, according to some historians in 935. Boleslav fights superior German armies for 14 years before submitting to the rule of the German kings who are now promoted to Emperors of the Holy Roman Empire. Bohemia is granted greater autonomy, Bohemia's western borders are defined and acknowledged, and Czechs are given a free hand in the East, provided they follow their conquests with conversions to the Roman Church. The Moravian Slav rite, however, is still tolerated and taught freely in some parts of Bohemia and Moravia. Boleslav's conquests reach the Carpathian mountains to incorporate Moravia, Silesia, Slovakia, Krakow, and Ruthenia.

***

# The Slavnik Massacre

To make sure their sovereignty over all Czech tribes remains unchallenged forever, the Premyslids under Boleslav II decide to get rid of the second most powerful clan, the Slavniks, who independently rule their territory in in north-eastern Bohemia. The family still adheres to the Slav rite, but one of their relatives, Vojtěch (Adalbert in Latin) had studied Latin theology and is now bishop of Prague, later to be canonised.

One of the early chronicles, written by Prague deacon *Kosmas* in the 12th century, recounts the event of a September day 995:

"Choosing a festive day, they stole into the Libice castle while Saint Vojtěch's brothers and their castle guards were celebrating holy mass. Like savage wolves they climbed the castle walls and slaughtered every man and woman, beheading Saint Vojtěch's four brothers in front of the altar before their children's - eyes, set the castle aflame, sprinkled the streets with blood, and burdened with their bloody loot, they merrily returned home."

That day, 28 September 995, is regarded as the day on which the united Czech state was founded. The Premyslids were helped in this by the third most powerful clan, whose name few remember now because they were all slaughtered in the same way shortly afterwards. Bishop Vojtěch flees to Poland, where he is murdered two years later. The clan exterminator earns himself the nickname Boleslav *Pious*. This establishes the Czech tradition of giving nice nicknames to nasty people, in the hope that it would make them nicer.

He is also known as the pioneer of good Anglo-Czech relations: His first wife was Princess Adivea, daughter of an Anglo-Saxon king whose name the Czechs can't remember except that it started with an E. It could be any one of seven who were ruling England for short spans and siring nubile daughters around that time.

\*\*\*

# Carry on Premyslids

Having thus brought unity and pious peace to their land and established forever the borders of the historical Czech crown lands, the dynasty goes on ruling for over three centuries without first making too much of an impact or achieving anything memorable on an international scale, but gradually becoming a scourge to all Central Europe, which is forced to repeat over and over their unmemorable and unpronounceable names as they swap bums on the Czech throne and acquire new territories.

Wrap your tongue around them.

Jaromír, Oldřich, Jaromír again, Oldřich again, Břetislav, Spytihněv, Vratislav, Konrád, Bořivoj, Svatopluk, Vladislav, Bořivoj again, Vladislav again, Soběslav, another Vladislav, Bedřich, another Soběslav, Bedřich again, another Konrad second-named Ota (setting a family flair for double names), Václav II, Přemysl Otakar I, Jindřich Břetislav, Vladislav Jindřich, Přemysl Otakar I again and this time promoted to king for all generations, Václav I (yes, this cancels out the earlier Václavs who were only princes), Přemysl Otakar II (the *iron and golden king*, who becomes so powerful that German princes have to join forces to get rid of him), Václav II. And finally teenage Václav III, whose murder in 1306 after only one year's reign ends the Premyslid male line.

Exercising power over the Czechs and neighbouring tribes for five centuries, the Premyslids leave behind several major towns named after them, including Poland's *Przemyszl*, Silesia's *Wroclaw* (*Breslau*), and Slovakia's *Bratislava* (both named after Vratislav), Mladá Boleslav (now famous for its Volkwagen-Škoda plant), and several dozen smaller ones.

What a family.

***

# Moravian Field

Also known as *Marchfeld*. One of the battles which Czechs regard as a national disaster, caused in no small measure by the treason of some Czechs. The battle which halts the expansion of the mighty Czechs under the *iron and golden king* Premysl Otakar (also known as *Ottokar*) II in 1278, and marks a reversal of fortune for the Czech kingdom.

By mid-13th century, PO2 is the single most powerful of the seven electors of the German Emperor, and his Czech Kingdom the largest of the Empire's constituent states. It is precisely his power, though, which prevents him from being elected (losing the election twice). German electors, dreading not only PO2's absolute power, but probably even more the prospect of having to learn Czech, would rather be ruled by an innocuous German-speaking weakling. So they proceed to elect an obscure upstart Swiss baron named Rudolf Habsburg. So scared are they of PO2 that they don't even inform him of the election, let alone invite him.

The first thing Habsburg demands as Emperor is that PO2 returns Austria, which he had acquired 25 years earlier as a youngster by marrying the 50-year old heiress of Austria's ruling family whose male line had died out. Although by now blessed with a younger wife, PO2 believes his early marital sacrifice has paid amply for such an insignificant piece of land as Austria, and gives RH an unequivocal two-finger sign (which, in that neck of the woods, is actually a one-finger sign).

RH responds by having PO2 excommunicated by the Church, which forces the aristocracy to withhold allegiance from their king. This is obeyed not only by the Austrian aristocracy, but also by some south Bohemian nobles, who see it as their opportunity to loosen PO2's grip.

In 1276, RH invades Austria and drives PO2 out, with the support of Austrian aristocracy. Two years later, the deeply insulted PO2 tries to take Austria back. This is how a Czech chronicler describes PO2's last battle:

"Lances are trembling and fields and meadows are soaking blood, some men are being slaughtered, others chased and caught like birds, most are dying by the sword. Like thieves, many Czechs seek safety in flight and disgracefully abandon their king surrounded by enemies, with only a handful of the faithful fighting gallantly. But as the resistance of a handful against the many cannot last long, the king is taken prisoner and against all dignity of the Empire immediately executed."

And king Rudolf's own deeply regretful account:

"Abandoned by almost all, he still could not retreat and resisted, with his giant spirit and morale, with admirable courage, until several of our knights threw him, mortally wounded, with his horse to the ground."

Some 12,000 Czechs fell there, in the ignominious *Moravian Field*.

Austria lost, Habsburgs the new horses to watch for.

Their rising power is resented at both ends of their empire. The other one is Rudolf's own homeland – where they remembered the Habsburgs as the naughty boys who pulled flies' wings and beetles' legs, stoned birds, and stole neighbours' chickens – and where the first three Schwyz cantons join up to resist Habsburg rule as the core of the future tiny but brave and indefatigable Switzerland.

The last two Premyslids, Wenceslas II and III, redirect their powers northward, eastward, and – carefully bypassing Austria – southward, until their reign stretches from Gdansk in the Baltic, Lublin in East Poland, Poznan and Krakow, Bohemia, Moravia, Slovakia, Hungary, Croatia, and down to the Dalmatian coast.

\*\*\*

# The Most Coveted Distaff

A massive scramble for the oh, ever-so-lovely Premyslid women breaks out after their last man's death. The still teenage deceased Wenceslas III leaves four sisters (ages ranging from 2 to 16) and one young auntie, his father had left behind a teenage Polish wife. Dukes, princes, and kings go berserk over them, including the two-year old Agnes who is betrothed to some Polish or Hungarian pederast by the time she's five. If you've forgotten what these men are all after, turn back to the first page of this book. Plus, of course, the prospect of one eighth, or one quarter, or a half, or God knows maybe even the whole of the Premyslid inheritance, now a prized possession. An industrialised and fertile country with industrious folk and the richest silver mines in Europe.

First, a minor German duke Henry Carinthian marries Ann and gains the reputation of a kind man with the Czechs, who elect him as their king. To the Czechs, "kind" has always meant someone who lets them get on with their business, treats their crimes and peccadillos leniently, and generally does not bother them too much. This Henry certainly did, since he had no idea what the hell was going on in his kingdom.

Second, Rudolf Habsburg's seventeen-year old sickly grandson prince named Rudolf Habsburg (no kidding) marries Wenceslas II's eighteen-year old widow and Wenceslas III's step-mother Elizabeth. She is a foreigner herself, so as far as the Czech nobles are concerned she does not count, however much she might still be their last queen. Under pressure and bribes from Rudolf's father Emperor Albrecht I, however, enough Czech nobles switch loyalty from Henry to Rudolf. Albrecht declares the Czech throne as lapsed in favour of the Empire and himself as the sole executor, giving himself the right to pass the

Czech throne to any one of his six other sons should Rudolf not survive. This, of course, breaks every rule in the book, and should have served the Czechs as a fair enough advance warning about the Habsburgs' ethics and ways of getting things done.

The Habsburgs tried a *blitzkrieg* on Bohemia in 1304 and had to retreat with the loss of 30,000 men. Now they are ready to have another go. Rudolf invades Bohemia to claim his throne but dies in July 1307 before he can engage in battle. An unfounded rumour has it that he was poisoned.

Some Czech nobles re-affirm their throne to be the rightful inheritance of the Premyslid women, and call back Ann with Henry Carinthian, who had left without putting up much of a fight against the Habsburgs, and still has no idea what the hell is going on in his kingdom.

Other Czech nobles, who remain pro-Habsburg and anti-Premyslid, back Rudolf's brother Frederick Habsburg who is after Wenceslas II's daughter Elizabeth, the step-daughter of his brother Rudolf's wife also called Elizabeth. He has, in the meantime, also tried to invade Moravia and woo it away from the Czechs.

Something pretty close to a civil war breaks out between pro-Carinthians and pro-Habsburgs, which the pro-Carinthians win after a couple of massacres in Prague and Kutna Hora, the main silver mining town.

Henry Carinthian, still having no idea what the hell is going on, returns to the throne, having made some shaky alliances with minor anti-Habsburg dukes and counts.

The Habsburgs invade again, father and all brothers together, this time succeeding to do a lot of plundering. Before, that is, Emperor Albrecht gets murdered by his nephew John of Austria, who also happens to be a grandson of Premysl Otakar II, nephew of Wenceslas II from his sister Agnes' marriage to Rudolf

Habsburg (the first one), and cousin of Wenceslas III and his oh, ever-so-lovely sisters, exceedingly pissed off that he has been completely left out of the scramble for his grandad's estate. That he happens to be a Habsburg and a Premyslid at the same time is one of the finer twists in this story which you can no doubt still follow with ease.

After this, the fast-expanding Habsburg house of cards collapses and takes a while to recover. Their invasion of Bohemia disintegrates and Frederick renounces his claim to the Czech crown "forever" in a "gentlemen's agreement", for the price of 45,000 talents of silver, payable within two years. Modest price, really, for giving up something that never belonged to him in the first place.

Thus Henry Carinthian becomes the ruler of one of Europe's great kingdoms and still doesn't know what the hell is going on. Nor does he ever find out, and Czech aristocracy uses this to acquire powers unprecedented anywhere. They set out to plunder the royal purse by giving themselves the privilege to manage the state budget, including income from the extremely lucrative silver mines, gradually taking law into their hands, settling their own disputes with the sword, until Bohemia becomes an ungovernable country where no one who owns a weapon leaves home without it, as a chronicler of the time puts it.

It is into this state of lawlessness that skillful Czech diplomats behind the scenes arrange a marriage of the stunningly beautiful and remarkably mature eighteen-year old Elizabeth (Wenceslas III's sister, not his Polish stepmother) with a fourteen-year old handsome boy called John of Luxemburg, son of the newly elected king of the Roman Empire Henry VII of Luxemburg. This establishes a Czech penchant for alliances with nations that are far away enough to have no territorial desires on the Czech kingdom.

As of 1310, the Czechs have a new dynasty with a Premyslid woman at the top and are on the way to greatness the likes of which they had not imagined in their wildest dreams.

Henry Carinthian packs up again and leaves without ever having discovered what the hell was going on in his kingdom.

*** 

## Battle of Crécy

This is John Luxemburg's famous last battle where, fifty and blind, he rides into battle on France's behalf against the English, to be praised as the greatest fighter of his time by none less than England's Black Prince. This is 28 August 1346, ending John's glorious expansion and defence of the Premyslid realm, and ushering in an almost entire century during which no one dares take up arms against the Czechs. His new conquests include Silesia, Lusatia, Goerlitz, and parts of Italy.

Great fighter, gallant knight, shrewd diplomat, but dreadful statesman, John is constantly getting into trouble with the Czech aristocracy, who have got used to too much of the power share and aren't prepared to give it up. Unable to rule without them, he leaves domestic politics to his wife, who soon gets used to her husband's coming home only when he needs more money to throw into battles and a wholesome lay to sire three sons and four daughters before she dies in 1330.

So restless and bored with his bad-mannered uncouth and ungovernable Czechs does John get that when there is no battle to fight for his own crown, he roams the battlefields of Europe to fight for his allies, of whom France becomes the main one. "No major battle can start without King John" becomes an unwritten rule among Europe's knights.

By 1337, John hands over the rule of his entire kingdom to his son Charles, who has a unique flair for governing, building, learning, arts, sciences, and industries, inherited from his mother and refined by the best teachers in France and Italy. The Czechs have been catapulted out of their Middle-European parochialism onto the great European stage, soon to become one of its most important centres.

The battle of Crécy is the first major battle of the hundred-year war between England and France, and King John, at fifty, blind for several years, uses it as a gallant way of ending his life by honouring his alliance with France. No Czech interest is involved in this battle, but Czech volunteers are there, alongside a Luxemburg contingent, defending France against England's King Edward III's army which lands on France's northern coast on 12 June 1346 and marches on Paris, plundering the countryside.

Crécy is where the two armies engage on the hot day of 26 August, and although the French and allies outnumber the English at least two to one, the English have brought with them 2,000 archers whose arrows have a longer range than the French traditional strongbows, and cull French cavalry and infantry before they could get anywhere near man-to-man combat. France's and allied casualties are counted as 11 princes and dukes, 2,000 knights, and 30,000 infantrymen.

King John's unit is reported by retreating eye-witnesses as charging against the English while everyone else sees the battle as lost and is running away. Only 100 knights join John in his gallant suicide. None of them survive.

"Never shall God witness the Czech king run away from battle", is the last line Czech legends put into their bravest king's mouth.

***

# Praga Caput Regni

Whatever John's son Charles was (and he was a lot of things to a lot of people), he was not a late starter.

Married at seven. Sorbonne graduate at thirteen. Governor of 17 Italian towns at fifteen. General of armies, builder of fortresses like Monte Carlo, and friend of poets like Petrarca at sixteen. Duke of Moravia and builder of castles at seventeen. King of Bohemia and of Rome at twenty. Founder of the first Central European university, urban designer and city builder at twenty two.

Nor was he an early stopper. He sired twelve children with four wives, the last one at the age of sixty with a wife 31 years his junior who is reported to have bent iron bars and broken swords and horse-shoes with her bare hands as her daily work-out routine before breakfast. He used most of his children for building powerful alliances instead of fighting wars by marrying them off to potential enemies and indifferent strangers. These included England's Richard II who got Charles' ever so lovely daughter Ann.

On accession to the throne, Charles swiftly makes mutually advantageous deals with the powerful Czech aristocracy – which, apart from providing an internal modus vivendi, bring desperately needed cash to the royal kitty drained by his father. He legislates Czech as a lingua franca alongside German and Latin. Mobilises for the one and only unavoidable war but wins it without a fight when his chief enemy breaks his neck falling off a horse on a hunt a couple of days before fighting is to commence. Avoids many more wars through clever diplomacy.

Charles achieves greater privileges for the Czech kingdom than are those of the German constituents of the Empire, with Czech nobles retaining the right to elect their own king rather than have him appointed by the Emperor and the Pope. Czech is what he decides to be and make the best of, and puts all his cosmopolitan education and experience at his country's disposal in every way he can.

He makes Prague the capital of the Holy Roman Empire, brings in the best builders, architects and artists he can find at a price he can afford to pay, designs a sevenfold expansion of Prague to almost twice the size of Paris to accommodate 40,000 residents, provide work for 10,000 workers and craftsmen, and turn the city into Europe's biggest building site of the century.

The design Charles gives Prague is monumental enough to serve the city's expansion and needs for six centuries, till the industrial revolution. He involves nobles, merchants, and craftsmen in the construction by selling them plots of land in the New Town on the contractual condition that the new owner has his building design approved to fit the overall urban style and needs before he acquires the site, starts to build within one month, and moves into a completed house within eighteen months, on pain of severe fines for default.

Instead of travelling out to the big world, Charles has the big world come to him. Over 400 painters make a living in Charles's Prague. In proportion to its population, this would equal 100,000 painters making a living in London or New York today. By mid-century, Prague has 104 churches. It runs 20 Latin parish schools, 4 collegiate schools, 3 monastic schools, and 1 Jewish school – four times the Empire's urban average per capita. The university has 7,000 students, of whom 80% come from abroad, mainly German states, Poland, and Hungary – given that Charles's is the only university east of Paris and north of Padua.

Expanding trade routes and building new short-cut roads, Charles is even toying with weird designs like a canal linking the Elbe and Danube rivers.

CAROLVS·IV
IMPERATOR
ROMANVS
PATRIAE
QVE
PATER·

AD OCCIDENTEM

Throughout the country local arts and industries flourish, new vineyards and orchards are planted, culinary arts refined, first cookery books written. A typical celebratory dinner party in the King's household, with the participation of archbishops, dukes, counts and artistic celebrities, consists of anything up to thirty courses of delicacies which include river fish, game, venison and wild mushrooms, washed down with gallons of local wine, by then sufficiently refined to please the King's Italian-trained palate. Well, just about.

"It's a bit rough," he comments on it in one of the stories handed down by a fellow drinker, "just like the Czech people".

Committed environmentalist and dedicated mushroom picker, Charles legislates against the destruction of forests in a way that would make him Greenpeace's pet.

"As the beautiful chain of our forests inspires the admiration of foreigners, we wish not only to stop their wastage but we intend to spare them all felling. Wishing to preserve them untouched and eternal, we decree that none of our foresters and game-keepers, nor any other person, may fell trees, transport them out, purloin or sell, other than wood already dead dry, or such trees as have been felled by the winds. Whosoever contravenes this edict, does so under the threat of having his right hand chopped off." A very humane punishment for his time, by the way, since he also outlaws a number of the then customary legal practices like chopping off noses, cutting out tongues, or plucking out eyes.

Whatever Charles IV may have achieved as an individual, and whatever his real driving force was for doing so, no one before had done so much to help the Czechs reach for the highest stars of glory – and almost, almost get there to stay.

\*\*\*

# Bible Against Church

By the end of the 14th century, the Roman Catholic Church has become the biggest and most crooked monster business the world has ever seen, squeezing cash out of everything and everyone. Owning a third of Europe's land, the Church is the wealthiest land-owner and keeps growing. Celibacy, imposed on the clergy, makes sure no cleric's or monk's property can be inherited by anyone other than the Church. Land-owner's taxes, collected by every parish, now include not only a prescribed amount of produce, but an additional "smoke tax" on every fireplace in the house.

Bohemia and Moravia have one of the densest networks of Church agents and money-collectors operating in more than 3,500 parishes under the title of priests. In 1393, the Pope declares a "summer of mercy" on residents of the Czech lands. This entails a full remission of sins in return for a minimum of 15 visits to a Prague church, with confession (for a fee) each time. The final sin remission, however, comes only after you have given one of the churches the amount of cash corresponding to the cost you would have incurred in the previous "summer of mercy" if you had made a pilgrimage to Rome. The cost of that pilgrimage is assessed by specially appointed priests.

A huge turnover comes from "fines" for sins admitted to in confessions, and "remission notes" or "indulgences" issued by the Pope and sold in the streets as certificates of forgiveness of your sins.

But the greatest and smartest money-spinner is set in motion when the Papacy discovers it can charge its priests huge rentals (appointment fees) for their parishes, bishoprics, and archbishoprics. From now on, bishops and archbishops are not the best theologians or men of the highest qualities, or even the shrewdest among priests, but the highest bidders. To pay the appointment fees, priests have to squeeze more money out of their parishes. The smarter priests buy several parishes and priestly appointments and then rent them out or re-sell them at a profit to other priests, or keep them while employing young assistant priests to do all their work for a pittance. There is a record of a Prague archbishop named Puchnik (the name means "stinker", quite incidentally) who owns and draws rent from 9 parishes while running the archbishopric.

Corrupt priesthood becomes the easiest route to worldly riches. The Church has reached the peak of the money-spinning game, without producing any wealth which would be to the benefit of anyone other than the Church.

And then the bubble bursts as the impoverished and God-fearing masses are told by a growing gang of hippy preachers that things don't have to be that way. That the Bible teaches something very different. And yes, folks, we are translating it into Czech for you. Read it, or come to listen. God's truth is with us. So are good songs. And terrific slogans.

The Church is the Antichrist. What a slogan to get a revolution going.

Prague becomes the hub of a theological revolution fired by Czech students returning from Oxford armed with John Wycliff's contraband books and his explosive statement "all depends on whether we put truth first or second". The revolution, which gains the sympathy of King Wenceslas IV, is run from pulpits by charismatic young preachers, of whom the best known and most influential becomes John (*Jan*) Hus, their most prolific Bible translator, Wycliff exponent, sermon writer, university professor, and Czech language codifier, who goes the whole hog and lets himself be burned at the stake in 1415.

S·KNIHAMI AŤ·JE·OPA-
TRNÝ·KDO JE·MÁ·NEBO
BUDE A I N SMÍTI
HVS

MAGI
STER

VERITAS

ARCIHERITICVS BOHEM:

His trial and execution is no mean event. The spectacularly stage-managed show lasts 8 months and is attended by "3 patriarchs, 23 cardinals, 27 archbishops, 106 bishops, 343 university masters, 28 kings and princes, 676 nobles, squires and knights", an eye-witness chronicler reports. He does not even bother to count the crowds of common folk who come to have a peep at the greatest heretic of their time. He does, however take the trouble to quantify the roaring trade done by "350 merchants, 170 taylors, 106 bakers, over 500 musicians and street comedians, and 718 hookers". Yes, 718 hookers. Not "at least 700", not "about 720," as most reporters would put it. Some fun he must have had counting them.

The execution enrages Czech and Moravian nobles to the point of drafting and delivering to the Church council a tough protest and warning note:

"We hereby testify to you and the entire world that Master John Hus was a righteous man devoted to God's law, teaching peace and love to us and all Christ's faithful. We also testify that whoever claims that there is heresy in the Czech lands is a liar, traitor, enemy of our kingdom, and a heretic himself. We are determined to defend our teachers of Christ's law to the last drop of blood, setting aside all fear."

Master John was not only a righteous theologian. He was also "one of us". The stake which burned him happened to be in Germany. All his judges were treacherous foreigners. A theological argument gradually turns into a national war, taken up by preachers, university lecturers, nobles, burghers, and peasants alike, all now reading their Bible in Czech. And to show they mean business, Czech priests begin to share their communion wine with their congregants, and replace the cross with the chalice.

Soon enough, the Czechs turn their righteous fury into the joy of making themselves a prime pain in the arse to the mighty ones of the mediaeval world.

\*\*\*

## God's Warriors and Joyriders

"Ye who are God's warriors, upholding His law, plead for God's help, and put your trust in Him, for with Him, ye shall always triumph".

Thus proclaims the Hussite anthem which, when sung by a 10,000 strong Czech peasant army choir and reverberating through the countryside, is enough to make any crusaders' armour rattle with fright even before the Hussites appear on the horizon. And its next verse becomes the powerful slogan which holds the invincible army together, marching on, and charging against the mighty armies of the Holy Roman Empire:

"Fear no enemies, never mind their numbers".

This inspires a generation of brilliant strategists and dedicated warriors, recruited from among country squires and farmers, fighting with weapons made out of farming tools. Using farming carts with light artillery, the Hussites in effect invent tank warfare which wreaks havoc on traditional crusaders' cavalry and infantry.

The 15 years of Hussite wars mark a period of the greatest national self-confidence and self-esteem Czechs have ever known, based on sound philosophical thinking and high ethical standards, and a firm belief in the righteousness of their cause, which gives them strength to keep fighting and winning against odds and without allies.

Czech nobles refuse to acknowledge as their king Sigmund Luxemburg, King of Hungary, King and Emperor of Rome, younger brother of the recently deceased Czech King Wenceslas IV, second son of Charles

IV, now officially appointed King of Bohemia. They regard him as a foreigner hostile to the Czech and Protestant cause. Which, indeed, he is. For a while, they are joined by the Polish and Lithuanian aristocracy from whose ranks they hope to elect their new king, and with whom they have some common interest when Teutonic Knights begin to pester Poland.

Five crusades led by Sigmund and joined by just about every European ruler are dispersed and driven out of Bohemia by Hussite armies, backed up by a growing number of Czech nobles adopting the Hussite faith, as well as Bohemian cities.

Such a military success is their defence of the realm that when no crusaders happen to be invading Bohemia, Czech battle addicts drive out on joyriding sprees through Germany. Partly to preach the Protestant philosophy creating fertile ground for Luther, partly to loot and collect ransom from besieged towns. Some of these drive as far as German Baltic ports.

Finally defeated at Lipany in 1434, exhausted, with their national economy in ruin, kingless and craving peace, the Czechs – by now overwhelmingly Protestant – agree to negotiate with the Catholic powers and allow Sigmund back on the throne, on the condition that he agrees to abide by a 4-article treaty with the nation, represented by the Hussite army, Czech nobles, and Prague burghers.

Under this treaty, the Czech kingdom becomes the first country where each and every resident is guaranteed a full right to chose between Catholic and Hussite affiliations. The Catholic clergy loses its right of representation in regional assemblies, while landed gentry and cities acquire it. A three-tier social system is formed of aristocracy, landed gentry, and burghers, which keeps the king in check – and which, with a stretch of imagination, could be called the grandmother of parliaments.

JSMENÉM·PÁNĚ

A delicate truce is established throughout the kingdom and whole Hussite regiments, with nothing better to do, sign up as mercenaries in Sigmund's army defending Hungary against the Turks. Many German settlers decide to leave, some are even expelled from a number of Hussite-ruled towns. Much of the land acquired by the Church is requisitioned and apportioned between the aristocracy, landed gentry, and towns. The peasants, who have done most of the fighting, can go and stuff themselves.

This truce, however, does not last a whole year before King Sigmund commits wholesale breaches of the treaty, threatens Prague's Hussite archbishop, and hangs one of the Hussite generals. All three estates rebel, Sigmund has to flee again and dies on the way to Hungary in 1437.

By now, the message is clear to everyone:

The Czechs will not be mucked about. They will elect their kings from now on.

They have also learnt a useful lesson:

You don't get what you deserve but what you negotiate. And you don't get what you negotiate if you don't grab it fast and defend it like a lion.

Shame they keep forgetting it over and over again.

\*\*\*

## Mediaeval Democracy

Having survived without a ruling king for a generation, it is almost surprising that the Czechs did not go all the way and think of establishing a republic on the Swiss model. And having already had some early unpleasant experience with the Habsburgs, it is amazing that the first king they should think of electing is Albrecht Habsburg, Duke of Austria, Sigmund's son-in-law.

Luckily for them, he dies two years later. To show just how imaginative they are, they elect another Albrecht, this time the Duke of Bavaria, who tells them to stuff their crown. The fact is, no one is too excited about the prospect of ruling the pig-headed Czechs.

Another twelve years of kinglessness, and still no republic. Still believing they must abide by some hereditary rules and regulations, the Czechs bring to their throne Albrecht Habsburg's 13-year old son Ladislas who dies on them four years later in 1457.

Suddenly – and no one understands why – the big scramble for the Czech crown starts again:

The King of France offers his son. Emperor Friedrich III offers himself. Casimir of Poland applies. Willam Duke of Saxony proposes.

Those long years that passed, however, made the Czechs realise they had to be ruled by one of their own. They tear up an old decree which stipulated that family ties and dynasty affiliations had to be observed in royal successions, and which effectively cut the Czech aristocracy from accession to the throne. After a lot of careful behind the scenes plotting and a brief mobilisation in the streets of Prague, the Hussite-backed temporary regent George (*Jiří*) of Podebrad is elected King of Bohemia, which then includes Moravia, Silesia, and Lusatia. He comes from the lower aristocracy, and some malicious Catholic tongues even claim he was his father's out-of-wedlock fling product.

This all-Bohemian election enrages the aristocracy in all the other Czech crown lands who were not consulted, a fair number of whom would still rather have gone for a foreign Catholic king like Matthias of Hungary. George proves to be a brilliant diplomat, and having convinced the grumbling Moravians and Silesians that his rule is in their interest, he gives his daughter in marriage to the Hungarian king and marries other relatives off to the dukes of Saxony and the Hohenzollerns of Brandenburg. Having appeased most of his immediate neighbours, he begins to rebuild his devastated kingdom.

Full observance of the Hussite-Catholic toleration treaty is George's domestic policy throughout the realm. To the rest of Europe, he presents a draft of a multilateral treaty on the settlement of conflicts between states and for a multinational organisation which would oversee peaceful co-existence and European security. The Hussite ideas were only a century ahead of their time. George Podebrad's vision of a European Union would take five centuries to be given a whirl.

It doesn't take the Vatican long to brand King George and the Czechs as heretics again and start another crusade. Hungarian king Matthias uses it to take Moravia and have himself elected Czech king there. Ailing George prepares a succession treaty with the teenage Polish royal prince Vladislav Jagiello.

On George's death in 1471, the Czechs are split between two kings who have no option but to fight it out. Neither of them can muster a strong enough army to defeat the other one, so they work out an elaborate compromise whereby Vladislav is the king of all Czech lands de iure, while Matthias remains the de facto ruler of Moravia, Silesia and Lusatia, with the proviso that whichever survives the other takes the lot and pays a compensation to the other's successors. Luck turns out to be on Vladislav's side when Matthias dies in 1490 with no male heirs, thus no one to pay to.

A paragon of simplicity, Czech politics, aren't they just.

Vladislav, although a Catholic himself, never intended to get involved in domestic religious squabbles on either side, and soon wishes he had never got involved with the crazy Czechs at all. All he ever wanted was to please everyone, make friends and agree to everything. To the Czechs, who love nicknames, he soon becomes "King Okay".

As soon as he takes over the whole country, Catholic aristocracy, having received a boost from Matthias and believing Vladislav to be on their side, try to stage a takeover. This is sussed out in time to be pre-emptied by the Protestants in a Prague anti-Catholic uprising which includes another jolly defenestration.

The toleration treaty is finally accepted by Catholics as inevitable (for now) and remains in force as law of the land until they get strong enough to break it again.

In the meantime, however, the unceasing Czech revolutionary itch moves from the religious sphere to the social one, and fighting breaks out between the aristocracy and the towns, right across religious affiliations.

Thoroughly peeved, King Vladislav gives up, packs his bags, and moves to Budapest. Bohemia becomes technically kingless again, as the next two generations of its rulers can't be bothered to visit Prague.

The Czech aristocracy discover new ways of turning land ownership into profitable business by setting up large cattle farms, fish lakes, timber and paper mills, textile and leather industries, and breweries – and make themselves stinking rich. With the need for new skills, more peasants become craftsmen, and more burghers turn into merchants – and make themselves stinking rich. More investment requirements produce more banking and stinking rich bankers. More people start craving better education. More books get written and printed, more art work is commissioned, and more buildings are built, as the Czechs cautiously and somewhat belatedly toddle from the austerity of the Middle Ages into the pleasures of the Renaissance.

And find they are probably at their best when left without any rulers breathing down their necks.

\*\*\*

## Enter the Habsburgs

And stay. To be followed by Habsburgs. And Habsburgs, Habsburgs, and more Habsburgs, endless streams of Habsburgs. Seventeen of them, and 400 years of them.

Having married Ludovic Jiagiello's sister, Habsburg Archduke Ferdinand finds himself overnight king of Hungary when the 15-year old Jagiello king gets himself killed in Turkish battles in 1526. Technically, that makes him also King of Bohemia, where, however, he still has to be elected. The Czechs, having no one better on offer (or so they believe, only to discover a century later that almost *anyone* would have been better, come to think of it), go through the motion of electing him. And if we don't count the three-month "Winter King" Frederic a century later, this turns out to be their last royal election ever. For the Habsburgs have by now established a habit of cleaving to other people's thrones and never letting go. Until now dukes of a minor country called Austria, they have acquired two kingdoms with strong economies and military prowess which they can now throw against the Turks and move for further land acquisition in the Balkans.

All right, so it doesn't look too bad for the Czechs to begin with. With Turks pushing into Hungary and all the way to Vienna, someone has to co-ordinate defence. Although sending armies to the battlefield, the Czechs are never directly exposed to Turkish conquest like the Hungarians, Slovaks, the Southern Slavs, and the Austrians.

RUDOLPHUS

REX
BOHEM·
ETC·

II
IMPE-
RATOR
AUGUS-
TUS

They get on, relatively undisturbed, with the business of developing the confederation's strongest economy, which they already were before joining up. A major build-up of towns and country residences gets underway, designed by Italian architects who imprint a new style not just on Prague and the Moravian capital Olomouc but on just about every market town which can afford it – and many can.

It is this period which creates urban architectural gems like Český Krumlov, Telč, Kroměříž, Třeboň, Jindřichův Hradec. It is also this period which brings the Czech aristocracy to their creative artistic and literary peaks, and ushers in a golden age of Czech literature. More Czech books get written during this period than at any time before or for another three hundred years after. Schools are set up in every small town, printing houses in every market town, and home libraries become the passion and pride of every self-respecting squire and merchant with a room to spare. The wealthier ones compete in library sizes, which reach 11,000 volumes in the homes of families like the South Bohemian counts and fish-lake magnates Rosenbergs (or *Rožmberks*, as they prefer to spell their name at the time).

A full and linguistically rich Czech translation of the Bible is printed in Moravia under the sponsorship of the Protestant Brethren Union. A second university is established in Olomouc in 1573 – though this one is exclusively Catholic. In an unprecedented explosion of learning, creativity, business, and tolerance, hatchets are buried for a while not only between Protestants and Catholics, but also between Bohemia's and Moravia's Czechs and Germans. Czech Protestantism grows into three branches:

a) Utraquists (moderate former Hussites making a compromise with the Catholics and recognised by the Habsburgs – at least temporarily, for comfort's sake),

b) Lutherans affiliated with the German Protestant church,

c) the Brethren Union which grew out of the more radical and ideologically uncompromising Hussite wing, now the most diligent promoter of Czech language, education and national culture, aware of the threat of germanisation, and feeling more cultural affinity with Holland, England, and France than with the German Lutherans.

Ironically, the still relatively comfortable religious tolerance in the Czech lands becomes the prime cause of increased germanisation, as thousands of German Lutherans move to Bohemia and Moravia from Austria and Catholic-dominated German states. Strengthening their numbers and setting up more German-speaking towns, they feel no compulsion to learn Czech, which at that time is still the official language of the kingdom.

In 1583, art and science lover Emperor Rudolf II moves his headquarters to Prague and makes it once again the Empire's glorious capital and a major European centre of learning. Czech physicians carry out the first ever full surgical autopsy and publish their findings for the benefit of medical science. Prague acquires scientists of the highest calibre, like astronomers Tycho de Brahe and Johannes Kepler. Under Rudolf's protection they work on ideas for which heretics are burned in Rome. For a while, Prague gives asylum even to the excommunicated heresiarch philosopher Giordano Bruno, before the Inquisition gets him and burns him in 1600.

For almost a hundred years, it looks as though nothing can ever go wrong for the Czechs.

But as the old saying has it, if you think you have no problems, you just don't know what the hell is going on.

And what's going on underneath the blinding renaissance splendour is this:

In 1527, central government offices are set up in Vienna with the power to overrule decisions taken by the Czech chamber of representatives. Czechs and Protestants don't seem to notice or mind. Nor do they seem to pay attention to what's coming next:

In 1547, after a defeated anti-centralist rebellion, Czech towns and aristocracy lose some of their privileges. Autonomy of towns is curtailed and royal governors – exclusively Catholics – are appointed to administer them, with armed police units at their disposal. Financial penalties are imposed on towns, and a royal court of law is established which can overrule all municipal courts. Many nobles, mostly members of the Brethren Union, have their assets confiscated. Two representatives of Czech towns and two Czech squires are publicly executed in Prague Castle square.

In 1556, the Jesuit order is brought in and establishes a well-organised educational network preparing the ground for a Catholic take-over.

Full Catholic pressure becomes tangible when the Spanish-educated Rudolf II becomes King in 1576 and moves to Prague in 1583, along with a large number of Spanish and Papal ambassadors, advisors, and consultants skilled in the promotion of the Catholic faith. Rudolf decrees Catholicism to be the only permitted religion, first in Hungary. Before he can do the same in Bohemia, Hungarian Protestants rise up in arms and drive the Imperial army out of Hungary and into Moravia. The Czechs, who one might have thought should by now be alert enough to see a potential ally, chase Hungarian Protestants back to Hungary instead.

In the meantime, Czech Catholics, who represent only 15% of the population, are promoted to all the highest offices in 1599. This is in effect a state coup which forces Czech Protestants to join up against Rudolf with his brother Matthias. Rudolf gives a free hand to Bavarian armies to come in and pillage Western Bohemia all the way to Prague. Czechs force Rudolf to resign in favour of Matthias in 1611.

Having helped him to the throne, Czech Protestants expect Matthias to back them. Wrong again. At the other end of Europe, a truce which held between Protestant Holland and Habsburg Spain for twelve years breaks down, and Catholic powers, of which the Habsburgs are the driving force, are on the move again to re-catholicise what they can grab. Bohemia becomes a decisive battlefield by 1617.

After the 1618 Prague defenestration, all four Czech lands (Bohemia, Moravia, Silesia, and Lusatia) mobilise, hoping that Protestants from other Habsburg-ruled countries will join. Few do. The Czechs go it alone and elect a new king, in the person of the Protestant Frederick Palatinus. His wife is the daughter of King James of England, whose support the Czechs hope to enlist. As always, Czechs expect too much of England. But it is at an English ambassador's banquet that the Czech king is given the news of his loyal subjects being massacred by foreign Catholic armies at a hill a couple of miles away from his table. He packs up and takes French leave the following morning never to return, forever to be known as the "Winter King", having reigned for one winter. His English wife keeps signing as Queen of Bohemia for the rest of her life.

What happens on that hill two miles away from Frederick's dining table turns out to be the greatest disaster in Czech history, which traumatises the nation to this day.

***

# The White Mountain

*Bílá Hora* hill is half-way between Prague Castle and the airport, now a pleasant suburb with a beautiful park and a small star-shaped renaissance chateau, a favourite meeting place of dissidents in the eighties. It must have had an almost pilgrimage effect on them, as if they were trying to absorb the aura of the place to understand their own "White Mountain syndrome".

The very sound of the name sends shivers through most Czechs' subconscious minds and emotions, and that includes today's Catholics. It has come to symbolise what the Czechs regard as their most self-sabotaging psychological pattern that paralysed them for three centuries, repeated itself in 1938, again in 1948, and yet again in 1968. It would, many suspect, repeat itself again under similar circumstances, and indeed repeats itself every day in Czechs' individual lives on a smaller and less visible scale.

Defeatism, lack of self-confidence, low self-esteem, the absence of clear strategic thinking in critical moments, feeling of being abandoned, fear of open self-expression, flair for back-stabbing and betrayal of one's own friends and allies when things get too tough to bear, tendency to leave things unfinished and give up hope, inner conflict between what they passionately feel to be right and what they reason out to be prudent, "if only" approach to situations, desire to cocoon up and blot out unpleasant reality instead of facing it and changing it, and the fear of being found out. In short, this is the psychological pattern which has the power to turn Czechs into quitters before they give themselves a chance to be losers. Before they can even notice what is happening to them, or understand how it happens.

Every Czech recognises the syndrome. Many acknowledge it as the single most powerful pattern subconsciously programming their actions to this day. Few have been able to identify its components and analyse it, let alone heal it. A detailed knowledge of this syndrome can be – and has been – a powerful weapon in an enemy's hands. If there is something with which the Czechs need a friend's help, this is it.

Many Czechs believe that their crucial historic battle was an act of enormous bravery in which gallant Bohemian and Moravian squires fought like lions, only to be defeated by great odds and treachery after a long and valiant struggle. That it was, above all, the hardy Moravians who resisted to the last drop of blood and would have rather died than surrendered.

The facts are much less flattering.

Some Moravian units did indeed resist to the last man, because they were so badly placed they had nowhere to run. Almost everybody else had, and did.

To begin with, the defending armies were not exclusively Czech. They consisted of Protestant units from German lands brought in by King Frederick and Hungarian Protestant cavalry, as well as the Czech Protestant Estates army. The chief commanding officer was a brave but foolhardy twenty-one year old German Protestant Prince Christian Anhalt.

Nor were they so badly outnumbered. An army of 21,000 stands a very good chance against an army of 26,000, particularly if strategically well situated – which it was. So well, in fact, were the Protestant armies placed that had they gone on the offensive at the right moment, they stood a fair chance of turning the Imperial and Catholic League army into mincemeat. Moreover, the Catholic armies were tired from a long march through Bohemia. They consisted to a large extent of poorly motivated mercenaries. One of those, records tell us, was a young and as yet unknown French philosopher called René Descartes, who certainly was not a passionate enthusiast of the Catholic cause. He just couldn't resist the chance to visit Prague all expenses paid.

It is here (or at around this time, at any rate) that Descartes receives the impulse to identify the *res cogitans*, or mind, with the human soul or consciousness, and to hold that everything has a cause, nothing can result from nothing, all matter is in motion, matter does not move on its own accord, the initial impulse comes from God, to postulate the dualism of mind and matter we call *Cartesian*, you know the stuff. Shouting *cogito ergo sum*, he runs straight off to Holland to avoid having to argue with the Church.

The November 1620 battle was a culmination of a fast two-month ignominious and incomprehensible no-resistance retreat from all defensible positions which the Czech Estates had held for two years. The battle itself – to the attackers' great surprise – was a walkover lasting two and a half hours.

The Czech king elect Frederic had been such a bad diplomat that he messed up relations and alliances with the entire Union of German Protestant States, whose rulers had decided a few months earlier to break off with him. Lutheran Saxony, in fact, goes as far as betraying its co-religionists and joining forces with the Emperor in return for a piece of the Czech kingdom. Other German states had made a pact with the Emperor not to come to the Czechs' aid at the crucial moment. The Czechs can't help construing this as one of the many examples of German perfidy.

In their enthusiasm for the Protestant revolution and joy that their two centuries old ideas have finally caught on next door, the Czechs fail to understand that Protestantism is by its very nature nationalistic. That in a conflict of interests, its nationalist nature overrides religious virtues like justice, neighbourly love, fair play, trust, honesty, and loyalty. That it does so just as unscrupulously as the Catholic Church sacrifices religious values to its overriding universalism and desire for disciplined uniformity.

Just as Hussitism became the driving force behind the Czechs' national confidence build-up and was the crucial weapon in their self-defence, so Lutheranism became one of the driving forces of German nationalism which had no interest in the continued existence of a strong Czech kingdom. Deep down, German Protestants felt more affinity with German-speaking Catholics than they did with Czech-speaking co-religionists. And the gullible Czechs found themselves sandwiched between – and crushed by – a Latin universalism of the Catholic Church, and a pan-Germanism of the Lutheran Church, both of whom agreed on one point: the Czechs were a pain in the arse they would both be better off without.

At the White Mountain, the Catholic commanders know that time is on their side and the Protestant rebellion is grinding to a halt. They even calculate that they can afford to sit out the winter at Prague's gates and starve the Protestant armies out, and they would, were it not for the personal ambitions of the supreme commander Prince of Bavaria who wants to earn himself some imperial chips on his epaulettes here and now.

The Commanders agree to do a small try-out attack from which they can assess the defenders' strength and determination. Two infantry squadrons and 1,800 cavalry men are sent to tickle the Czech Estates' left flank. To their own amazement, the second tickle makes the entire flank regiment run like mad.

Seeing their right flank flee, almost the entire 21,000 army take to their heels. There are only two

FERDINAND
II·VÍTĚZ
BĚLOHORSKÝ

MAJESTÁT

+16 21·

exceptions: One is the unit directly commanded by the pig-headed Anhalt, which gets itself slaughtered, with Anhalt taken prisoner. The other is the famous gallant Moravian regiment, which is so far back that they can't see what's happening, and whose retreat is blocked by a wall. Most of them are also slaughtered, with their commander Šlik, a seasoned and brilliant soldier, taken prisoner and later offered a good mercenary career in the Catholic armies of Albrecht Wallenstein, which he accepts with glee.

The strictly military causes of the disaster have been assessed as follows:

Ideological adherence to the more mobile Dutch method of fighting, against the traditional stiff Spanish method of the Catholics. This would have been extremely effective, if only – oh yes, "if only" – the Czechs had been properly trained to pull it off.

Compared with the Imperial army, Protestant mercenaries were poorly paid. Some 5,000 of them actually disobeyed the order to turn up for battle and stayed in the comfortable inns and the soft embraces of the oh, ever-so-lovely maidens of Prague.

And last but not least – or probably even foremost – there had been so many rows between the commanders over who was to do what when and why, that the soldiers were probably at a loss as to what exactly was expected of them – other than to get themselves killed.

The domestic national consequences of the White Mountain battle are worse than anyone could have imagined:

The Czech crown lands are taken over fully by Habsburg Emperor Ferdinand II immediately after the battle and hereditary succession is re-instated constitutionally, even through the female line, placing Habsburgs on the Czech throne forever.

Six months after the battle, 27 leaders of the Protestant uprising are publicly executed in the Old Town Square and their heads remain on display decorating Charles' Bridge gate for ten years.

A new constitution splits Czech crown lands into autonomous regions directly subject to the Emperor.

Autonomous privileges of aristocracy and towns are abolished and absolute rule of the Emperor is imposed.

German is legislated as lingua franca – on a par with Czech to begin with, later as the only official language.

The Catholic faith is decreed to be the only permitted Christian denomination. All Protestant churches are closed and their clergy expelled. An Imperial edict of 1627 orders all Czech aristocracy and townsfolk to convert to Catholicism or leave the country within six months. About a quarter of a million Protestants go into exile, their assets confiscated. The Brethren Union re-settles in Saxony, Prussia, Scandinavia, Holland, and England, and becomes known later as the Moravian Brethren.

Many Czech Protestant aristocrats are executed or dispossessed and their assets distributed among foreign (mainly German-speaking) Catholic supporters as a reward for their assistance. The Emperor expropriates some three quarters of Czech land and uses it as incentive and reward for loyalty. Right of residence and right to property is now granted exclusively by the Emperor, with no consultation with Czech aristocracy. Ten years after the White Mountain battle, approximately one third of all Czech land is owned by foreign newcomers, one third by Czech Catholics, and one third lies abandoned and fallow, waiting for more foreign Catholics to come and take it.

Catholic clergy are re-instated in top positions in the land chamber of representatives, over the aristocracy and towns. Large numbers of foreign Catholic clergy and monks are brought in to carry out thorough re-catholicisation of the country.

The highest political and administrative body – The Czech Office – is moved to Vienna to be run centrally, and alternative offices of central power with efficient bureaucracy are established in the three lands (Lusatia having been grabbed by Saxony).

Complete census of the entire population is carried out through parishes and direct taxation from Vienna imposed on all Czech lands.

Charles' University is handed over to the Jesuits and changes its name to "Carlo-Ferdinandian".

As the battles of the war roll back and forth for 30 years, almost half of the population is massacred, dies of starvation, or moves into exile, with less than 1 million remaining in Bohemia, just over 1 million in Silesia, and half a million in Moravia. Over 270 noble's estates, 100 towns, and 1,000 villages lie in ruins.

Large Jesuit colleges are established in Prague, Olomouc, and other major towns to turn out Czech-speaking Catholic clergy of which there is a dire shortage.

All education from primary school to university is Church-run and Jesuit-administered.

Many pre-White-Mountain Czech books are placed in the index of forbidden books.

In 1618, the population of Bohemia and Moravia was 85% Protestant. Within ten years, the ratio is reversed, with only a few small pockets of German-speaking Lutherans and Czech-speaking Brethren remaining in the regions bordering with German states and Silesia.

A new class of Czechs comes into being: an extremely unscrupulous, greedy, ruthless, turncoat and quickly re-catholicised group of quisling aristocrats and burghers who stop at nothing to grab as much of the ex-Protestant loot as they can. These number in all less than 1,000 men, the most powerful of whom becomes Duke Albrecht Wallenstein (*Valdštejn* in Czech). Ten years later, this infinitely ambitious man commands a loyal army of 35,000 and toys with the idea of re-taking the Czech kingdom for himself with the help of Sweden and Czech Protestant exiles, but is assassinated before anyone can find out whether he really meant it or was just playing treacherous games with both sides.

Internationally, the White Mountain battle has the effect of alerting all Protestant countries to the threat of the Habsburg pan-European conquest design, and makes them form an alliance consisting of Denmark, Sweden, Protestant northern German states, England, Holland, and the Catholic but anti-Habsburg France whose main enemy are the Habsburgs of Spain. The thirty year bloodshed ends with the Westphalian Peace Treaty in 1648 which stops Sweden and Czech exiles a few weeks short of re-taking the whole of Bohemia and Moravia from the Habsburgs.

The treaty rolls the Habsburg expansion back. All the Protestant coalition countries and France gain territory and security guarantees. The erstwhile brave and strong, and always rich and industrious Czech kingdom, birthplace of Protestant reformation, is written off, robbed of all its assets and treasures by whoever gets to them first, tossed to the Habsburgs as a consolation dog bone, and forgotten by friend and foe alike. Fifty years later, few recall it ever existed.

\*\*\*

## Exiles

The White Mountain drama opens up a new element in Czech history which is to remain its permanent feature to this day. It creates the concept of political exile, as opposed to migration for economic reasons. Czech exile never grows into a diaspora – on the Jewish, Irish, Armenian, or even Polish or Italian model. Once stuck out there with no chance or desire to return, Czechs usually blend into the background by the second generation at the latest. Their exile-born children become Americans, Canadians, Australians, Brits, Frenchmen, Swiss, with little interest in their ancestors' country or culture, and mostly with little or no knowledge of Czech. The rather amazing exceptions are a few Czech diaspora communities in Texas where eighteenth century Czech has remained the local lingua franca, and long forgotten great-grandma's cakes are baked today.

In the cruel dramas of the 20th century, exile patterns accelerate to four major waves in one lifetime. In the Czech nation – unlike any other – it creates a sore ongoing rift bordering on resentment and hostility. Between – as the "remainees" usually see it – "them who fled in search of a better life" and "us who stayed and suffered", or – as the expatriates see it – "us firm in our convictions" and "them who are bent".

There is one thing all Czech exile generations have in common: Within a few years of their separation, the thinking patterns and national feelings of exiles and remainees become so different that by the time they meet again, their ways of viewing the world and going about their lives are incompatible. The tragi-comedy of it is that although they still speak the same language – and many expatriates speak it better, with a degree of cultivated purity and richness – neither of them have any idea how come the words and sentences have taken on such diverse associations as to become mutually incomprehensible.

The expatriates – who settle mostly in countries with higher degrees of political, ideological, and entrepreneurial freedom, and lower degrees of moral corruption, gradually come to see their old country through their newly acquired parameters and standards. In a sense, they have refined the ideals and standards which made them leave their country in the first place. They adjusted them to – as much as having them molded by – their new environment. Such standards, in the meantime, have become obsolete – or at any rate inapplicable – in the old country where physical and material survival at all cost took priority over ethical purity of means.

This results in different rules of conduct governed by different aims:

Outside – the need to risk and adjust to material, social, and cultural discomfort, but in a free environment, results in a more idealistic, adventurous, flexible, confident, and open-minded approach to life. This carries with it acknowledgement of personal responsibility for success and failure alike.

Inside – the focus is on the struggle for the best achievable level of comfort under the circumstances as the only tangible safety feature. This takes priority over ethical purity of means, which is considered expendable and foolish. The result is a defensive attitude cleaving to whatever "small but secure" achievements there are to hang on to. As crooks and arse-lickers are seen climbing to the top, honesty and fairness become expensive commodities, dishonesty and spine-bending are seen to pay. Responsibility is relegated to "the system", in which it is impossible to succeed in any other way.

To both camps, their respective attitudes have become second nature which neither of them question – until they are confronted. Then all hell breaks loose.

Expatriates, in their idealism and belief they have a debt to pay to the old country, are perpetually frustrated and impatient whenever they try to help get things working to their standards. They end up being seen by the remainees as stuck-up, patronising, impractical, incessantly critical, never satisfied know-it-alls – for whom the Czechs use either the German word *Besserwisser* (spelt *besrvisr*), or the Yiddish words *Kibbitz* (spelt *kibic*) or *Eytzehgibber* (spelt *ejcegibr*). Those expatriates are disturbing their comfort.

So irritated do the remainees get that they frequently tell them to shut up or shove off. Absurdly, they end up siding with their former oppressors against those who have naively believed themselves to be their allies. This can even get today's Czech politicians to opine repeatedly that "expatriates have nothing to offer us, because they have not lived through it with us". It has even turned the once neutral Czech word *emigrant* into a swear-word for which amusing euphemisms are being coined.

Few realise that this, too, is a part of their White Mountain syndrome – which is ticking on, unnoticed, unanalysed, unhealed. From the White Mountain to this day, it has remained pretty much unchanged.

So let's have the gist of the first exile muster story:

The estimated quarter to half a million exiles (approximately one fifth to one quarter of the entire population) who start leaving in 1624 includes some of the nation's finest brains and talents which place themselves at the disposal of host Protestant countries. England's great acquisition is the engraver Wenceslas Hollar, famous for his panorama of London before the Great Fire. Sweden, and later Holland, benefit from the services of Europe's greatest educator of the time, Comenius (*Komenský*) who helps to restructure their education systems to make learning easier and more entertaining. Surprisingly, host countries include Catholic France and even Poland. And amazingly, the largest number of them settle next door in treacherous Saxony.

MUSEUM·LITTERARUM
BOHEMICARUM·PRAGÆ
BIBLIOTHECÆ STRAHOVIENSIS
AULA·THEOLOGICA·DICTA

Most of these people go into exile with the conviction that it is going to be a temporary arrangement which will end when the fortunes of war reverse in favour of Europe's Protestant powers. Many exiled Czech aristocrats and soldiers actively lead a diplomatic campaign against the Habsburgs. An exile Czech army is put together under Sweden's banner. They reconnect with their exiled "Winter King" Frederick who is living in Holland and whose word among influential people in Protestant countries still counts. He even toys with the idea of re-settling all Czech exiles in Holland or England, or even Ireland, and creating a second Czech homeland. Were it not for most exiles' craving to return home with a vengeance, he might have pulled it off, and Llanfairpwllgwyngyllgogerychwyrndrobwillantysiliogogogoch in Wales might be speaking Czech now. The name would have probably been simplified to *Krčstržbrdvlkprdlplžkrklmlžsrkl*, which means "shrubby steep forest hill where a wolf farted, a slug belched and a lamellibranch slurped". An altogether more accurate description of the place than the original "St Mary's church in the hollow of the white hazel near the rapid whirlpool of St Tysillio's church by the red cave".

Czech exile diplomacy is run by Count Vilem Kinsky who shuttles back and forth between Protestant countries' courts and embassies in an attempt to forge a large-scale anti-Habsburg alliance.

The military wing is led by a group of aristocrats headed by Count Henry Matthias Thurn who left in 1620 with the king. Resembling a foreign legion, Thurn's army seek every opportunity to fight the Habsburgs with anyone who has a common anti-Habsburg cause. In 1621, they join Hungarian Protestants in an attempt to push into Moravia. A year later, Thurn enlists the support of the Hungarian Protestant leader Bethlen. This gentleman commands a sizable army of Turks, Tartars, Hungarians and Rumanians which takes Slovakia and rolls into Moravia. To the Czechs'great disappointment, Bethlen lets himself be bribed into accepting a peace settlement just as he is about to smash the Imperial armies to smithereens in 1623. The following year, the indefatigable Thurn signs up as the Venetian Republic's chief *condottiere* in charge of all Venetian armies, hoping to bring Venice into the war. Thurn's grand view of the anti-Habsburg alliance includes awareness of the news that Cuba and Puerto-Rico have risen up in arms against Habsburg Spain. By 1627, Thurn's armies are fighting for Denmark, and a year later, they sign up under Sweden, with whom they stay till the end of the war, and where many of them are buried.

Count Thurn must have a charismatic effect on the Czechs, because he succeeds in recruiting most of the youngsters of the exiled aristocracy, burghers, and peasants into his army. Seasoned soldiers by now, Czechs fill some of the highest ranks and many of the middle ranks in the Swedish army. Unlike average mercenaries, these soldiers are highly motivated patriot fighters.

Their successes in the drive across Poland and Germany towards Bohemia and Moravia are acknowledged with admiration by northern German states, most notably Saxony, whose armies join in a Protestant push on Prague in 1631 – only to rob Prague castle of its treasures and betray the Czechs and Swedes again by helping to prevent a large-scale domestic Czech uprising organised by Thurn. This does not, frankly, require too much effort, since most domestic Czechs are so exhausted by now that they prefer to sit the fighting out and wait to see who wins, so that they can come out comfortably on the winning side. Ten years after the change of regime, the exiles' patriotic commitment is totally alien and disturbing to them.

To the exiles' amazement, large numbers of re-catholicised and well paid Czech soldiers are now fighting against them on the Habsburg side, led by Duke Wallenstein, the greatest and most unscrupulous megalomaniac in Czech history. They drive the Swedes out of Moravia and Silesia, Wallenstein takes Thurn prisoner, and begins to discuss a possible anti-Imperial alliance with the Czech exiles before releasing him against the Austrian king's orders but forcing him to order Swedish garrisons to vacate their positions in Silesia.

Wallenstein's promise of support is given when Thurn, on behalf of the exiled aristocracy, offers him the Czech crown. Whether the promise is truly meant to be honored, we shall never know. Wallenstein is assassinated in 1634 along with a number of Czech exiles as they are negotiating details of their collaboration.

The exiles conclude that they can now expect no support from inside the Czech kingdom, which can now be liberated only by an allied force of arms, almost against its own will. They now channel all their energies into Sweden's war campaign.

By 1645, they have re-taken most of Moravia, and join up on the Danube with anti-Habsburg Hungarians led by Rákoczi. In July 1648, in a surprising blitz attack, they take Prague Castle, and a few days later the South Bohemian towns of Tábor and Český Krumlov. As they are about to re-take the whole of Prague, their – and the Czech exiles' – triumphant victory is cut short by the Westphalian Peace Treaty.

Swedish armies retreat, and Sweden, once committed to obtaining full restitution for its Czech exiles, signs the following treaty on their behalf with the Habsburgs:

Czech and Austrian exiles may return home if they submit to the law of the land, i.e. convert to Catholicism. Expropriated assets will be returned to those from whom they were taken for reason of their joining Sweden's army – after 1630.

This excludes 99 percent of them, since most joined before. Rumours circulating in northern Germany have it that for this treaty, the Swedes have accepted a special compensation from the Emperor to the amount of 600,000 Imperial tollars. Sweden vehemently denies this.

But the betrayal of the Czechs is now complete.

No reply is given to Comenius' letter to Swedish military governor Oxenstierna:

"It is on behalf of many that I am writing this, moved by their laments, throwing myself at your feet again and through you at the feet of the most brilliant queen and the entire council of governors, I beg and beseech you by the wounds of Jesus Christ, not to abandon us who have suffered so much for Christ! Behold this people which, first among the peoples of Europe, was first blessed by Christ's mercy and wrested from Antichrist's darkness, which before other peoples received the light, suffered the fury and anger of Antichrist for a whole century. Hear this wretched people, so that you, too, can be heard by merciful God."

Political exile turns into permanent emigration.

Many similar events follow. Again and again, fighting exiles lose touch with the domestic population, which, in turn, loses the commitment to its freedom. Again, and again, Czechs are let down by their allies.

Never yet have they thought of asking themselves these questions:

What is it we are doing wrong that makes our friends to whom we have been so loyal turn their backs on us when we need their support most?

Why do we, again and again, place ourselves in a position where we are at the mercy of forces we cannot control?

What can we do to change this curse?

\*\*\*

## The Re-Awakening

This is the Czech equivalent of the Italian *Risorgimento*. Or rather would be, if the Czechs had a Garibaldi. They don't. Nor do they have a Cavour or a Mazzini. What they have instead is Radetzky, a soldier from a Bohemian village called Radeč, now a leading Austrian field marshal who makes himself famous precisely for fighting the Italian *Risorgimento* off, trying to prevent its re-unification with Italian provinces owned by Austria. He does so successfully for many years. (Yes, it is indeed he of Strauss' *Radetzky March* fame.)

With the rise of Italian and Hungarian nationalism in the early 19th century, the Habsburg kingdom slowly begins to break at the seams. The trouble with the Czechs is that by now they are living in a Bohemia and Moravia which is perilously germanised. Of its population of 6.8 million, more than a third have either never known or forgotten how to say vowelless words, let alone what they mean. But the Czech lands, German or Czech speaking, now densely industrialised, are again the most productive and industrious region in Central Europe, and Austria's economic backbone, producing 60% of its GDP.

In the century just past, Habsburg Empress Maria Theresia lost a couple of wars to Prussia and paid for them with a large chunk of Czech territory called Silesia – which by then had become densely germanised.

In 1749, she abolished Bohemia's and Moravia's joint kingdom status even on paper and incorporated both lands into Austria's administrative apparatus as separate regions, splitting the Czech nation down the middle.

Her son Joseph II couldn't be bothered to have himself crowned Czech king, and introduced some of the best ideas of the French Enlightenment, of which the best was: You can believe and think whatever you like, as long as it is in German.

Mozart chose Prague for the world premieres of *Nozze di Figaro* and *Don Giovanni*, claiming: "My Praguers understand me".

Emperor Franz introduced total and absolute power and a police regime in all Habsburg countries, but for some strange reason allowed the establishment of a Czech language department at the otherwise totally German Prague University.

Napoleon defeated Austria and Russia near a Moravian village called Austerlitz *(Střelice u Slavkova)*, after which Austria changed sides and let Napoleon move on to Russia, just to change sides again a few years later and join Russia and Prussia in the "Battle of Nations" at Leipzig, where the allied armies' commander in chief was a Czech marshal, Prince Schwarzenberg.

The first Czech nationalist clandestine organisation is established in 1844, choosing to call itself by the English name Repeal, and Czech things get moving again. Their March 1848 initiative, backed by the second nationalist organisation called St Wenceslas Committee, is a petition containing a few modest demands: The re-establishment of an autonomous administrative territory corresponding to the traditional Czech crown lands, Bohemia and Moravia. Equal status of Czechs and Germans in that territory in all walks of life. General abolition of serfdom. Municipal self-government. Freedom of the press, assembly, religious affiliation.

The Emperor accepts the petition on the language equality point but rejects the land autonomy and municipal self-government. Czech newspaper, periodical, and book publishing explodes nationwide, as literary Czech is taught fervently in every Czech-speaking village. A journalist and political satirist of Mark Twain's wit appears in the person of Karel Havlíček Borovský, to be silenced and sent to a comfortable exile in the Italian Alps for being a pain in the neck not only to the Viennese authorities but even to sentimental Czech nationalists who don't like being made to look like fools.

Czech poets, inspired by English Romantics, create their first masterpieces, of which two belong to European Romanticism's top class: Karel Hynek Mácha's *May* and Karel Jaromír Erben's *Bouquet of Flowers*. One of Prague's oh, ever-so-lovely young ladies called Božena Němcová writes a book called *The Grandmother*, which is to become a world-wide bestseller for a century. Translation of the best from English, French, and Italian literatures assumes a frantic pace as voracious Czech readers crave to keep their fingers on the pulse of European culture. Pre-White-Mountain Czech history is revived and studied. Czech theatre troupes roam the countryside. By the late 19th century, illiteracy is unknown among Czechs.

Czech leaders are invited to Frankfurt to join a pan-German federation against the Habsburgs. Finding that what the enlightened Germans have in mind is a total and final germanisation of all non-Germans within their reach, they decide to give full backing to Austria, stick with the devil they know, and press for some form of multi-national federation within the Habsburg Empire. With this in mind, they decide not to rock the boat, and do not join the 1848 revolution as wholeheartedly as the Hungarians or the Viennese. It is the Moravian town of Olomouc which gives asylum to Emperor Ferdinand V when the Viennese revolution threatens his life. And it is a Czech aristocrat, Count Kolovrat, who replaces the notorious totalitarian Metternich as Austria's Prime Minister after the 1848 revolution cools down.

In their newly found national confidence, most Czechs remain staunch supporters of the Austrian Empire as a fortress in which they feel fairly comfortable.

"If there were no Austrian state, we would have to make sure that, as soon as possible, in the interest of Europe, nay even humanity, it was created," says eminent Czech historian and national leader František Palacký in 1848. It is he who coins the concept of *Mitteleuropa* – as the territory lying between Germany and Russia, inhabited by small nations, defenceless unless joined by a strong Austrian Empire.

Twenty five years later, frustrated by continued Habsburg intransigence which he sees heading for a collapse of the Empire sooner or later, he gives up:

"We existed before Austria, we shall exist after it."

But by then, the downtrodden Czechs, tolerated by their German neighbours as rather silly and amusing innocuous pets, have transformed themselves into a modern confident nation determined to become masters in their house, waiting for Austria to self-destruct due to its own lethal mistake.

That mistake comes in 1914 when she triggers off an all-European war – as Germany's ally. This is seen as the final blow to any remaining illusions about Austria's role as protector of its small constituent nations.

By then, Czechs have enough seasoned and skilled politicians, diplomats, economists, bureaucrats, and soldiers to risk giving Austria a poke to help it down into oblivion. The illusion of and nostalgia for a continued comfortable, cosy, *Gemütlich Mitteleuropa*, with all its chequered ethnic and cultural blend, however, dies hard, even as erstwhile fellow citizens of the same country start reaching for each other's throats after the Habsburg roof has collapsed on their heads. And with it disintegrates a whole geo-political order which kept European affairs predictable and comprehensible, and in which wars were still fought by gentlemen with respect for their adversaries.

\*\*\*

## Months of the Century

The accelerating history of the 20th century finds Czechs simplifying their historical references by giving their critical events names of months.

The epoch-making ones are called October, September, March, May, February, August, and November – in that order. Most of the epithets which some of them used to have in addition – like "Victorious" – have now been dropped.

Most of these events are so close to the skin they may prove difficult to joke about.

\*\*\*

## October – 28th, 1918

The day on which the free republic of Czechoslovakia was proclaimed in Prague.

This, according to English Kabbalist Z'ev ben Shimon Halevi can in effect be taken as its birthday, which would have made Czechoslovakia a Scorpio – a lovable and loving, if slightly foolhardy and pig-headed creature with a strong flair for self-deceit and self-destruction. Even those who regard astrology, let alone one applied to nations, as a hocus-pocus gobbledygook pseudo-science, cannot have failed to notice how much of a self-destructive country Czechoslovakia was.

It was therefore very surprising, and even slightly worrying, that the 1-January-1993-born Czech Republic decided to keep 28 October as its official birthday. This, effectively, still makes it a Scorpio, and its self-destructive streak has not been removed. If, however, one counts 1 January as its actual birthday, that should make it a more stable and better balanced Capricorn, just like Slovakia, which was born on the same date in the Czecho-Slovak split. Continued celebration of 28 October could therefore have a long-term schizophrenic effect on its people.

Those who don't believe in astrology are referred to the traditional kabbalist astrological adage that astrological birth signs affect even those who do not believe in them, the only difference being that they don't know it, and have, therefore, no control over it.

Since the Czechs as a nation, and earlier Czech states as living entities, were born and re-born several times earlier on, it is quite possible that the actual birthday is on an altogether different date which we are no longer certain about. This would mean that we have no way of knowing what makes the Czechs tick, and it might be a good idea for Czech historians to start arguing which of those dates to choose and celebrate in the end, depending on the sign they want their country to be, in order to make it behave the way they want. It could bring some fun into the nation's otherwise currently rather monotonous money-focused lives. They have a good historical precedent in the astrologers, alchemists, and kabbalists of Rudolf II's time. English alchemists, astrologers, and kabbalists at that.

But as if that were not enough, Czechoslovakia was not born where everyone thinks it was – but in America. And not on the 28th of October, but ten days earlier, which would make it a Libra. For it was on the 18th of October in Washington that Masaryk proclaimed to all and sundry the birth of free Czechoslovakia, on behalf of the Czechoslovak government (himself, mainly), with an outline of the new country's constitution. The chief pediatrician was President Woodrow Wilson, who had rallied to the Czech cause only a few months earlier, in time to give the baby the final pull with the awesome might of the United States.

Thomas Garrigue Masaryk was for a long time (well into 1915) the only man who believed that dismantling Austria and setting up a Czecho-Slovak state was not only feasible, but desirable. He did not come to the conclusion himself until he became aware of an agreement between Germany and Austria which envisaged a closer integration of the two countries and full germanisation of Austria's nations. Both countries' chancellors, in fact, regarded the war as being predominantly between Germans and Slavs. This would leave the Czechs, most of whom considered themselves neither German nor particularly committed Slavs, with a choice of two camps, neither of which looked a tempting prospect. Unless, that is, they made a go of it on their own, looking for backing far outside the Central European arena in Western power, whose political model Masaryk felt suited his nation best.

Now well into an age when most people think of quiet retirement, Masaryk goes into exile in December 1914, and sets about the arduous task of explaining to Americans, Brits and Frenchmen who the Czechs are and what they want. And above all, how their renewed statehood could be to the benefit of the Allies.

"We are shamefully unknown out here," he writes back home to his small circle of anti-Austrian supporters who call themselves *Maffia* (yes, Czechs have a penchant for mis-spelling foreign words to make them look even more foreign). These count little more than a couple of dozen people, two of whom join him in exile. One of them is a skilled bureaucrat but a pan-Slavist pro-Czarist romantic, whom Masaryk promptly sends out of sight to Russia. The other is a thirty-two year old methodical hard-working beaver with amazing diplomatic skills and good Freemasonry contacts named Edward Beneš. It is he who gets Czech propaganda moving in the French and Anglo-Saxon press and influential circles.

To get the Slovaks involved, the exiles team up with a Slovak-born French army officer and scientist Milan Rastislav Štefánik who plugs them into French political circles, all the way to the top government level, and authorises them to use his name in support of their claim that "Slovaks are a branch of the Czech nation who use their dialect as a literary language". Just as importantly, he also gets them the financial backing of the American Slovak community. It is these three men, against all odds, who create a world-wide awareness of a "double-nation" which historians everywhere believe has been extinct for three centuries.

Back home, few people have any idea that this is going on, and fewer still would back it if they knew. Domestic Czech politics are firmly steeped in the idea of a federalised Austria, Slovaks are not even trying to stretch their imagination to the possibility of leaving Hungary and linking up with the Czechs. Prague is, after all, so much further away than Budapest.

The home-grown Czech mainstream political organisation calling itself The Czech Union, continues to claim till the end of 1917 that "the Czech nation, as always in the past, so in the present time sees its future only under the Habsburg scepter".

In the meantime, however, Czech and Slovak soldiers on Russian, Serbian, Italian, and French fronts are getting thoroughly peeved at having to die for an empire they no longer consider theirs, and go for easy capture and surrender by the thousands. It is from their ranks, plus expatriate volunteers, that Masaryk, Beneš, and Štefánik get the ingenious idea of creating a Free Czechoslovak Legion to fight on the side of the Allies.

By the summer of 1917, the Legions have become a military force to reckon with, totalling 85,000 men who know they have to fight to the last drop of blood because capture would mean death for desertion. Some 55,000 are fighting on the Russian front, 20,000 in Italy, and just under 10,000 in France. At the end of 1917, the National Council of Czechoslovakia – as Masaryk, Beneš, and Štefánik now call themselves – is recognised as the lawful representative body of the two nations by the government of France, followed soon by the USA, Great Britain, and Italy. After thee years of Masaryk's hard slog. Thanks to Masaryk, the Allies enter 1918 convinced that Austria must not only be defeated but also dismantled.

The first home backing comes from a manifesto of 220 writers, journalists and scientists in May 1917, but it isn't until early 1918 that domestic Czech politicians begin to toy with the idea of full independent statehood and start preparing themselves for it practically. But most Czechs are caught with their pants down when statehood falls in their laps from outside.

The bulk of the Legions in Russia get stuck in a Bolshevik revolution in which they first have an order not to interfere, but when the Bolsheviks try to prevent their peaceful departure, they go into full-scale anti-Bolshevik offensive to blast their way out of there through Siberia to the other end. For a year or so, they become the effective rulers of large territories of Eastern Russia, and their example inspires many a local anti-Bolshevik uprising. So successful are they as fighters and organisers that the Allies request that they remain there and link up with Russia's anti-Bolshevik forces to prevent a Bolshevik victory, which is now becoming a major peril. It is Beneš's diplomatic deal in exchange for this agreement that makes all Allies recognise the National Council of Czechoslovakia in September 1918 as the lawful government of the soon to be born republic. The Legions remain stuck there for two more years.

When Lloyd George is asked who achieved the greatest victory and got the best deal at the end of the war, he says, not altogether without tongue in cheek:

"Professor Masaryk."

The seeds of Czechoslovakia's self-destructiveness are planted at its very birth.

To start with, not only did the country's godfathers get the birthday wrong, they gave the country the wrong name. For not by a long chalk was Czechoslovakia a country of Czechs and Slovaks.

The mind boggles to know how come they did not think of the one and only logical ancient name uniting the two territories – Great Moravia. Calling themselves Great Moravians would certainly have been more acceptable to local Germans, Hungarian, Ukrainians, or Poles, than having to refer to themselves as "Czechoslovaks". It could have made the country into another Switzerland.

The more you think of it, the more absurd the name becomes. Few foreigners can spell it, fewer still can pronounce it, and those who can get it mixed up with Yugoslavia. Most only get to learn it at long last when it ceases to exist, and then they are surprised they got it wrong again. It is a difficult enough country to imagine, let alone care about.

The reason the godfathers faked the existence of a "Czechoslovak" nation (i.e. Czechs and Slovaks being "two branches of the same nation"), was to make sure that they would have a working national majority in the new republic. As Czechs, they could not be sure they would even get as far as 50%. They did – just. It was 51%. With Slovaks added in, they reached 65.5%.

In 1918, the 13.6 million population consists of 6.8 million Czechs, 1.9 million Slovaks, 3.1 million Germans, 750,000 Hungarians, 460,000 Ruthenians, Ukrainians and Russians, 180,000 Jews, 75,000 Poles, plus a few Rumanians and others. And although any ethnic group is by law entitled to use their language in official dealings in all districts where they constitute at least 20% of the population, the two main minorities, Germans and Hungarians, make it clear they are not prepared to take orders from neighbours whom, until recently, they were used to regarding as second-class citizens. In this, they have the backing of their co-nationalists across the border.

In Slovakia, incumbent Hungarian ruling structures refuse to vacate the country, and the Czech army has to move in to reclaim its internationally recognised territory. It is no match for the Hungarian army which goes on fighting until January 1919, when ordered to leave by Western Allies. A few short months later, Hungarian soldiers are back, this time calling themselves the Hungarian Red Army and spreading Bolshevik revolution following a Bolshevik coup in Budapest. The integrity of Czechoslovakia's territory on the Hungarian border is not re-established and guaranteed until July 1919.

Bohemia's and Moravia's Germans, now calling themselves Sudeten Germans, declare the establishment of autonomous provinces *Deutschböhmen, Sudetenland, Deutschsüdmähren*, and *Böhmerwaldgau*, two of which demand incorporation into Austria. The Prague government sends troops to occupy them and establish central government rule, without too much resistance. The incorporation into Czechoslovakia is to an extent welcomed by Sudeten German industrialists and businessmen who see the country's economic potential in its international acceptance.

Czechoslovakia becomes overnight the wealthiest country in Central Europe, inheriting almost 70% of the Empire's industry. With the disintegration of the Empire, however, it has lost its traditional guaranteed markets. The resulting industrial crisis, with unemployment rising to an unprecedented 200,000, takes four years to recover from. Restructuring its exports to overseas markets, Czechoslovakia hits the world's top twenty by 1927.

Communist and break-away nationalist undercurrents begin to gnaw from inside. Two German nationalist parties are established in 1919. The Communist Party is established in 1921 and gets almost a million votes in the next election, becoming the second single strongest party with 13.2% of the vote. In 1925, half a million Slovaks vote for Hlinka's autonomist and gradually separatist Popular Party. The Mussolini-style Czech Fascist League, led by a well known Legionnaire general, starts gaining publicity around 1925, but the highest support it ever gets is 2% of the vote. The Czechs are trying to take it all in their stride to the best of their democratic convictions and abilities. Given the circumstances, they are not doing too badly.

But Masaryk predicts that Czechoslovak democracy needs fifty years to put down roots.

Twenty is all it gets.

*\*\**

# September – 30th, 1938

Generally known as Munich. A symbol of ignominious international betrayal. Strong allies forcing a weak ally to surrender to the enemy without a shot. In breach of a defence treaty.

The domestic prelude to the event starts at the 1935 election, in which the avowedly pro-Nazi Sudetendeutsche Partei gets two thirds of the Sudeten German vote, and becomes the strongest single party in the country, with 15.2%. The other German parties remaining are the German Social Democrats and the German Christian Socialists who, both anti-Nazi politically, are at this stage still trying to work out some autonomous arrangements for the German-speaking regions within Czechoslovakia's democracy. German communists are all in the Czechoslovak Communist Party.

In 1937, an arrangement is indeed thrashed out which would seem to make sense both to the Prague government and the German-speaking regions. Were it not for the fact that SdP's chiefs Henlein and Frank are by now plotting something quite different on Hitler's directives: To go on presenting demands which they know to be beyond anything the Prague government could concede to.

In more than one speech, Hitler makes it clear that he considers it his duty to "liberate over ten million Germans living in adjacent states and secure them general freedom, personal, political, and ideological". From June 1937, the German general staff are drafting plans for a full invasion of Czechoslovakia.

With full knowledge of this, in April 1938, Henlein presents his notorious Carlsbad demands, which he emphasises are the minimum acceptable: Full recognition of Sudeten German national parity with the Czechs, establishment of a separate autonomous Sudeten German region with German self-government and full adherence to the German nation and the "German world view", national socialism. The Prague government replies with four successive offers in the next five months, all of which Henlein turns down. By now, "Home to the Reich" is most Sudeten Germans' slogan, as the remaining non-Nazi German parties resign from Prague politics and disband themselves, and Henlein's SdP gets 90% in Sudeten German municipal elections.

In May, Prague calls a partial mobilisation, determined to fight. In this, it still has the backing of the Sudeten German Social Democrats, as well as all Czech and Slovak political groups, including the small but vociferous Czechoslovak Fascist League and the Slovak Popular Party. The SdP attempt a coup on 12 September, which government forces put down.

Lord Runciman's mission, well briefed by Sudeten German chiefs on joint hunting trips, reports to London that "further co-existence of Czechs and Germans in one state is impossible". It is the by now inescapable truth of this statement that invests President Beneš's post-war policy of the expulsion of Germans from Czechoslovakia.

Britain and France draft a plan for the hand-over of districts with more than 50% German population, and present it to the Czechs on 19 September. With it, Czechoslovakia would give up its entire defence line, beyond which it would become indefensible. Czechs turn the offer down, but following further tough pressure from British and French ambassadors, Prague government agrees, but following massive street protests, resigns the following day, to be replaced with a new government led by a general. The country is bracing itself for a tough fight and mobilises on 23 September.

Hitler informs Britain and France that he shall wage an all-out war against Czechoslovakia if Prague does not fulfill his conditions by 28 September. Chamberlain notifies Hitler in writing that he "can get it all without a shot".

On 29 September, Hitler and Mussolini meet Daladier and Chamberlain in Munich, and shortly after midnight 30 September, sign a treaty ordering Czechoslovakia to hand over the Sudeten German territories peacefully.

Under additional threats of attacks by Hungary and Poland, Beneš calculates the unlikely odds of 1.5 million Czechoslovak soldiers winning a war against 3.5 million Germans, and against strong protests of all staff generals and the tangible upbeat mood of the nation, calls off the mobilisation, signs the treaty, resigns five days later and goes into exile.

It is only after Hitler inspects Czechoslovakia's fortifications that he realises just how lucky he was.

German Generals had calculated Czechoslovakia's odds as follows:

To break through Czechoslovakia's defences and defeat its army, they would have had to use thirty-five divisions. This would have left only five active and eight reserve divisions on Germany's Western border, against France's potential one hundred divisions. Czechoslovakia had the power to defend itself for at least one month, possibly six weeks. That time might have been enough for France to change its mind, walk into Germany, and finish it off.

The likelihood was they might have dissuaded Hitler from attacking if Czechoslovakia remained mobilised.

Beneš's surrender decision on 30 September is condemned by the Chairman of the Defence Committee on the same day:

"Excuse us, Mr. President, if we disagree with you. In this castle, Czech kings ruled an independent state and often determined European history. This castle has never known surrender. We should have defended ourselves. We have given up of our own will. Future generations will condemn us for surrendering our lands without a fight. Where should the nation seek strength and what should it believe in, when we have taken away its army, making it abandon its defence positions without a shot? Foreign cowardice has now been amplified by our own. It is true that others have betrayed us, but we are also betraying ourselves."

The fact that the Defence Committee and general staff do not dare relieve Beneš of his position of Chief of Staff and replace him with a military government is amazing enough. But that the same people accept him again a year later as their head of state in exile to lead them through the war and to liberation, makes the mind boggle.

And you might wonder again how come the Czechs are still not asking themselves:

What is it we are doing wrong that makes our friends to whom we have been so loyal turn their backs on us when we need their support most?

Why do we, again and again, place ourselves in a position where we are at the mercy of forces we cannot control?

What can we do to change this curse?

*** 

### March – 15th, 1939

"If we cannot sing with angels, we shall howl with wolves. If the world is to be ruled not by law but by power, our place must be where there is greater determination and power. Let us seek – for we have no better choice – an accommodation with Germany".

A public statement that breaks the nation's resolve and triggers its moral demobilisation. It is printed by a popular daily, Lidove Noviny, a few days after Munich, written by one of the participants of a meeting of ministers and generals at which the idea of a second line defence is discussed behind the President's back, but given up.

In the meantime, German armies occupy a third of the Czech lands to great cheers from the local population. Several hundred thousand Czechs, and some twenty thousand anti-Nazi Germans flee into the crippled remnant of Czechoslovakia, to join some ten thousand refugees from the Reich itself, who have been there for some years now. They have five months of freedom left before Germany closes in on them.

In a pathetic predatory gesture, Poland invades Northern Moravia and occupies a territory with a Polish-speaking majority, closes all Czech schools, and bans all Czech associations.

Hungary follows suit with an invasion of southern Slovakia and Ruthenia. The remainder of Slovakia declares autonomy and the name is changed to Czecho-Slovakia.

The map of Czecho-Slovakia now resembles a "corpse gnawed by hyenas and cut in two", and the Czechs, who thought of themselves as everybody's beloved pets, now gasp at the ferocious hate shown by all their neighbours.

The limbo in which the nation hangs for the next five months turns people into zombies, as they go about their business trying to blot out reality and thoughts of worse things yet to come. The government tries to soften the blows by bravely failing to introduce anti-Jewish measures and encouraging Jewish and political emigration. More than 20,000 Jews leave the country during these five months.

It sells some of its now unusable military hardware to foreign anti-Nazi organisations and opens a foreign account to finance future exile operations. Too much of it, however, still gets into Hitler's hands later. Politicians who would be likely victims of Nazi persecution are sent away.

Czech intelligence staff officers set up operations in London and a first-rate clandestine home network, preparing for an early occupation. They succeed in recruiting a prominent Nazi and high officer in German military intelligence who sells the Prague team top class accurate information from Berlin headquarters. Passing it all to London, they become a valuable asset in their exile government's war contribution. One of the early items their Nazi contact delivers is a warning of the exact date for the invasion of the remainder of Czechoslovakia. Among the many others is the date of the planned German attack on Great Britain, the date of the invasion of Russia, the locations of V1 and V2 bomb factories. A handful of Prague Czechs may have provided Churchill the crucial information which helped him save Britain. It was the same small group of Czechs to whom the House of Lords awarded special thanks after the war. Posthumously, in many cases.

Several thousand men cross into Poland, Russia, Rumania and onwards, to set up an exile army, which later reaches France just in time to put up a good fight against Hitler, and is pulled out just in time for the Battle of Britain.

A day before invading Bohemia and Moravia, Hitler forces Slovaks to declare independence or face a Hungarian occupation. The remainder of the Czech lands, already chopped down to 60% of their size, is occupied and incorporated into the Reich on 15 March. Edward Beneš – the man who ordered his army to surrender after Munich – now has the refined taste to express disappointment that not even a symbolic resistance was put up against the invasion.

The 170 precious Czechoslovak airmen, pilots, navigators, and mechanics who got away in time, shoot down 158 German aircraft in the battle of France and 340 in battles over Britain, make 148 bomb raids on Germany, and knock out 6 submarines and one battleship.

Well organised, small, London-linked resistance and sabotage networks continue for three years till reprisals after Heydrich's assassination in May 1942 wipe out most of its activists. With the exception of the intelligence network, organised resistance almost dies down.

By now, some 80,000 Czech informers are listed by the gestapo. As concentration camp sentences are imposed on black market dealers and even farmers who fail to declare a pig, goat, rabbit, or hen, people in villages start settling their personal scores by denouncing their neighbours for just that. This is not a good time to be getting on someone's nerves.

Most young men are sent to Germany as slave labour in factories, farms and on building sites. Many don't return. Concentration camps are filling up not just with illicit goat-owners but with many intellectuals, writers, journalists, and educators whom the ruling Sudeten German butcher and ferocious Czech-hater Karl Hermann Frank labels as the cause of all that disgusts him about the Czech nation. All Czech universities and colleges are closed down.

In the whole of six years, not a single Czech writer of any importance writes a pro-Nazi book, play, article, or poem. Not a single film director of any importance makes a pro-Nazi film.

But by the end of the war, the nation, many of whose leading figures have not survived, smaller by a quarter of a million dead, is so exhausted with the struggle for survival and so demoralised that it becomes like clay in the hands of the communists who manipulate it, bit by bit, to exactly where they want it.

After all, most people think, nothing that can come now could be as bad as what we have just survived.

Well, of course it isn't.

You don't get taken away for owning a goat.

The goat does.

***

## May – 9th, 1945

Yes, for the Czechs, the war ends a day later. Prague SS and gestapo units must have got so attached to the oh, ever-so-lovely maidens of Prague that they had to be blasted out of there by a couple thousand poorly armed Czechs, with the help of the Vlasov army. These were Russians fighting in German uniforms who switched sides on the last day and ran to surrender to the Americans and Brits. Little good did it do them, they were all shipped back to Stalin to be shot. But they did save a few hundred lives and a few dozen beautiful buildings in Prague.

Following closely behind Soviet tanks proper (a week, to be precise) arrives a Czechoslovak government of a so-called National Front whom no one elected, headed by a president who once resigned and hasn't been re-elected, with a political programme thrashed out between London and Moscow (but mainly Moscow). It promptly brushes aside the Czech National Council of domestic resistance leaders and excludes them from power. It nationalises all large businesses. It outlaws the Small Entrepreneurs Party which used to poll just over 5%, and the main conservative party with a long name called Agrarian for short, which used to pull in almost 15%. Ostensibly because one or two of their members collaborated with the Nazis, but mainly to get rid of right-wing democratic opposition and swing Czechoslovak politics sharply leftward and into the firm embrace of Soviet liberators. Beneš, moreover, never forgave the Agrarians for having had the audacity to put forward a second candidate for the Presidency against him in 1935, and now is his chance to get even in a big way.

The Agrarian party, as the name might suggest, had its strongest support among farmers. Finding themselves politically homeless and trying to avoid being accused of siding with quislings, these numerous farmers have four parties to chose from now:

The Catholic People's Party – a centre party which gets the support of some of the more successful farmers who also happen to be Catholics.

The National Socialist Party – a centre party which gets the other successful farmers who do not happen to be Catholics, plus all the Small Entrepreneurs.

The Social Democrats – moderate left party which gets one or two of the intellectuals among farmers.

The Communist Party – which gets the bulk of the less successful ones plus some of the successful shrewd ones who know how to back the winning horse. It also gets all the smaller pro-Nazi informers, collaborators, interrogators, and similar scum who can't find a better place to hide. The communists make good use of them later. By the first post-war election in May 1946, after a full year of brilliantly organised communist propaganda in the country, communists have by far the largest majority.

A true and typical story of that time from a Moravian village:

A communist propaganda preacher gives a three-hour lecture on Marxism to local farmers in the local village hall. Finishes and opens up "question-time, comrades".

"Yes, comrade", an elderly farmer stands up, "may I thank you on behalf of all of us here for your brilliant and exhausting exposé. Everything seems to be crystal clear to me, and I have only one question, comrade. Is Marx also inhabited?"

The voting figures in the 1946 election in the Czech lands, compared with the last pre-war parliament, in which there were also some 10 other parties, are as follows:

Soc. Dem.: pre-war 12.6%, post-war 15.58%
Nat. Soc.: pre-war 9.2%, post war 23.66%
Peoples': pre-war 7.5%, post-war 20.24%
Communist: pre-war 10.3%, post war 40.17%

The balance of power within the National Front parliament is 56% on the left, 44% in the centre, zilch on the right. And the constitution does not allow any political parties outside the National Front coalition.

To put this into perspective, Czechoslovakia was no more communist than France, Italy, or Greece. But it didn't have the luxury of de Gaulle, the Mafia, or the colonels. What it did have and they didn't was a common border with the Soviet Union and a network of Soviet agents who stayed behind when the liberating armies went home. And, above all, except for a small strip of western Bohemia, it did not have the intense emotional experience of being liberated and pampered by fun-loving gum-chewing Americans and the always cheerful Brits.

In the next two years, the communists will have replaced most police chiefs, top army officers, and key media personnel, having obtained the ministries of Interior, Defence, and Information. And they will have collectivised some two thirds of agricultural land and facilities, having also obtained the Ministry of Agriculture. The Trade Unions, now also communist-run, set up their own paramilitary and well trained force called People's Militia.

Suddenly, everybody is a resistance fighter. Issuing bona fide resistance certificates and testimonies becomes good business, as the communist-run Anti-fascist Fighters Union turns into an important para-political force. The country's poets, from the greatest rhymers to the meanest scribblers, compete to see who can write the most syco-phantic verses praising Stalin and the Red Army.

Everybody professes sincere adherence to socialism or democratic socialism, socialist democracy, or peo-ple's democracy. No one dares criticise the commu-nists or the Soviet Union. Those few who do are, well, not yet exactly threatened, but pilloried in so many publications that they soon feel the whole nation is against them, and realise they have just put their name on someone's shit list. If a newspaper, journal, or pub-lisher fails to please the communist ministry of infor-mation, the ministry fails to give it enough paper – which is under its strict control.

On the surface, everything looks hunky-dory, as Emil Zátopek wins every long distance track event in sight, Jaroslav Drobný reaches the finals at Wimble-don, the Czechoslovak ice-hockey team wins all the matches there are, and Tatra and Škoda cars are still a great buy. To the Western Allies, the Czechs appear, as always, perfectly lovable democrats. So what if they are getting so friendly with the Russkies, some-one's got to, and you can't really blame them after Munich, can you, poor darlings? After all, look at all those English girls who married the Czech pilots and soldiers and now live there with them? They've got to be all right, haven't they, dear?

And something else happens:

Between the first day of peace and the end of 1946, over 2.5 million Sudeten Germans are expelled – "ho-me to the Reich". The Potsdam Treaty's official word is "transfer".

"To liquidate the German question in our country," is how Beneš presents his ethnic policy in his first speech on Czech soil on 12 May. Because "the German nation ceased to be human in this war, and appears to us as a single enormous human monster."

Before orderly government-organised transfers can begin, gangs of rogue vigilantes, thieves, hoodlums, gold-diggers, and something calling itself Revolutionary Guards, have three months of free hand for a wild robbery and killing spree throughout Sudetenland. The number of Germans who died during this period has been estimated by teams of dedicated Czech and German historians at around 30,000, Sudeten German sources claim more. In just one report from the north-Bohemian town Usti nad Labem, 400 Germans, including women with babies, are beaten to death, shot or drowned in a single day by Czech crowds run amok. All Czech murderers and robbers of Germans are subsequently amnestied by Beneš's presidential decree of 1946. A nasty streak in the Czech psyche has come to the surface, to horrify and haunt many of those Czechs who otherwise support the transfer itself.

It has become fashionable to claim that the transfer was all engineered by Stalin, as part of his plan to get the Czechs under his thumb. This may sound logical to the revisionist ("Nazism was nothing more than Europe's reaction to Bolshevism") and relativist ("it was no worse than Bolshevism, and is therefore judged unfairly") lines of thinking which have been gaining ground for some time among German historians and journalists.

The documented facts, however, indicate that the first suggestion of a transfer was made by Czech domestic resistance some time around the time of the reprisals following Heydrich's assassination, in which many Sudeten Germans participated with glee. It was at their suggestion, though fully in accordance with his own post-war picture of the country, that President Beneš made the transfer an integral part of his policies. At first he thought of a transfer of Nazi supporters only (difficult to prove each case individually among 3 million), and finally he decided on all except proven anti-Nazis, those remaining loyal to the Republic, or those married to Czechs. This would leave about a quarter of a million allowed to stay. In the end, fewer did.

Beneš received American approval for this idea even before he presented it to Stalin, who, of course, wholeheartedly supported it, may have even helped fine-tune it, and offered to guarantee Czechoslovakia's western borders. It was agreed by Allied powers and made part of the Potsdam Treaty in 1945. The legality of the decision was supported by the fact that the vast majority of Sudeten Germans did, shortly after annexation and then invasion, take the citizenship of the invading German Reich, thus renouncing their Czechoslovak citizen rights. This is quite apart from the argument of whether or not their overwhelming support of Henlein's Nazi policies does or does not constitute high treason.

It has also become very popular among Czech flagellants to argue with a straight face that it was precisely the transfer itself (not just the criminal acts of wild-cat vigilantes) which set the Czechs firmly on the slippery road to Stalinism and crimes against its own citizens which were to follow three years later. The transferred Germans were – this is worth quoting verbatim – a "democratic core which would have resisted, nay even prevented, communism to take roots." And that therefore, logically, nothing but a full reversal of Beneš's post-war decrees – and the Potsdam Treaty – resulting in the Sudeten Germans' right to return, will save Czechs in the 1990s from the continued danger of slipping back into communism and Russian hegemony.

If the Sudeten Germans, with the assistance of the Czech flagellants, really mean to win the campaign for their right to return after fifty years, they will have to come up with better slogans. Something that sounds less Germanly logical and more absurd.

Most Czechs, and many war-time allies, probably still recognise that just as "further co-existence of Czechs and Germans in one state was impossible" before the war, as Lord Runciman had decided then, so much more did it continue to be impossible after. Nor is there any reason to believe it would be possible fifty years on.

Historically, from where they are standing, the Czechs cannot help seeing the transfer as an unpleasant but unavoidable curtains down on the seven or eight centuries of playing fair and generous hosts to a community of *Gastarbeiters* who were welcomed by Czech kings to settle in the Czech kingdom but who abused their hosts' hospitality over and over again, trying to turn them into second-class citizens in their own land – several times to a point which threatened the very existence of Czechs as a nation. There is nothing in the tone of the new Sudeten German campaign that would assure the Czechs that they have anything else in mind this time around. The least an outsider – and this might reasonably include mainstream Germans – can do is to acknowledge the Czechs' legitimate fear of this risk being renewed. They have enough problems to chew on without it.

Instead, it is with a gasp of amazement that Czechs watch the Sudeten Germans' demand for restoration of their Czech citizenship dragged up fifty years later by Germany's mainstream politicians, making it a Czech obstinacy issue and an obstacle to a co-existence treaty. It is with utter disbelief they hear the same politicians hint that this issue could even become an obstacle to Czech EU membership. It is with a sense of irony that they see the Germans plastering them with collective responsibility for the transfer, while at the same time disclaiming (rightly, of course) their own collective responsibility for the war and the Holocaust.

Germans have many great qualities, but tact and sensitivity to the feelings of others are not ones they are likely ever to be famous for.

Not to worry, though.

In their transformation into true capitalists, the Czechs are losing the ability to laugh at themselves. So much so that they are even unaware that this is happening to them. By the time they notice, it will be too late. As far as they are concerned, everything is for real this time. You are either seriously committed or seriously angry. Their politicians are pompous and humourless. So are their journalists. No one tells jokes, no one takes the micky out of anyone, least of all themselves.

Given a little more free-market time, the Czechs might make good Germans yet.

\*\*\*

## February – 25th, 1948

"The Victorious".

And deep down, all sincere Sudeten Germans are surely praising God for getting them out of there before this happens.

The penny drops in the summer of 1947, when Czechoslovakia's government – including the communists – accept the Marshall Plan and are promptly summoned to Moscow to be told that this would be regarded as an act of hostility to the Soviet Union and treated accordingly. Stalin has other economic plans for them. On his return to Prague, Foreign Minister Jan Masaryk says:

"I went to Moscow as the minister of a sovereign country and have returned as Stalin's lackey."

And privately, to some of his best friends and London exile associates, he gives the advice to get out while they still can. He even helps many of them to posts at foreign embassies. A visible trickle of soon to be emigrés start arranging extended foreign visits.

All the way to this moment – or possibly beyond – the vainglorious President Beneš has sincerely believed that he is a better chess-player than Stalin, and that Stalin will live up to his promises of Czechoslovak independence – because he owes him a favour. Yes, to him, Beneš, personally.

By February 1948, communist interference in the running of the country without consultation with the rest of the government, particularly in replacements of police staff, has become so blatant that the other three parties' ministers try to force an early election before it's too late. Half of the government hand in their resignations in the hope that the entire government will be constitutionally dissolved.

But the Prime Minister – a Moravian hoodlum and drunkard called Klement Gottwald – has another constitutional trick up his sleeve. For some years now, he has had his own stooges planted in the leadership of all three parties. He now uses these to replace their parties' ministers who have just resigned, and presents this new government to the President as a perfectly constitutional government re-shuffle to "prevent a political crisis and civil war". This set-up retains the two non-partisan ministers, Jan Masaryk in Foreign Affairs and general Ludvik Svoboda in Defence, both of whom have agreed to stay on.

By now, armed People's Militias have taken over major factories and offices, supervise a signature campaign for the peaceful hand-over to the new government, and march menacingly through the streets. Very few fail to sign. Police begin to arrest student activists. Almost 12,000 students march to the Prague Castle in support of the President who is still refusing to sign the new government. They are stopped by almost equal numbers of police and People's Militia and beaten up, with 118 arrests.

The President calls in Defence Minister General Svoboda and asks if he can rely on the army to defend the Republic. This is worth noting: The President, who is constitutionally the Commander-in-Chief, asks his second in command if he "can rely on the army", instead of ordering him to use the army, and having him arrested if he refuses. The trouble is, by now, there would probably be no one left to do the arresting anyway.

"I will never order the army to go against the people," replies Svoboda, whose long-term secret Communist Party membership now comes into operation.

Realising there is no force left in the country to defend democracy, Beneš signs the government reshuffle, gets fatally ill, retires to his country residence, resigns in June, and dies in September. Jan Masaryk, the last democratic minister left in the government, is found dead, having fallen out of a window on 10 March. Less than two weeks after the government reshuffle – which is in effect a communist coup d'état achieved without so much as a fistfight.

Half of Czechoslovakia's national ice-hockey team defects following their silver medal win at the Winter Olympics. Some 25,000 people follow, many others get arrested or shot trying to cross the border. Passports are made invalid and new ones have to be applied for. An electrified barbed wire fence and minefield strip soon separate the country from Germany and Austria.

Moravian hoodlum Gottwald takes up presidency in July with these proud words:

"Behold the first working-class president in the castle of Czech kings!"

And behold the Czechs do indeed. So much do they behold their beloved President Gottwald that they promptly – though very, very privately – nickname him "the greatest heart transplant surgeon of all time", for having "transplanted Europe's heart into Asia's - arsehole".

Others note how he discovered that the earth is round: "Shat on the West, got shit back from the East".

Czechoslovakia's democracy is officially re-named a "people's democracy". And Czechs soon find out that "the difference between democracy and people's democracy is the same as that between a jacket and a strait-jacket".

For a long time to come now, jokes will be the Czechs' only islands of sanity in a sea of madness.

"Buy him a new encyclopedia," says a friend to Mrs. Gottwald, who ponders what to give her husband for his birthday.

"Encyclopedia? He wouldn't know how to ride it."

Gottwald's response jokes include:

Full nationalisation of industry and trade.

Forced collectivisation of agriculture.

Censorship of all publications.

Social Democrat Party swallowed in a merger with the CP, turning thousands of decent democrats into communists overnight (most of those who resign lose their jobs).

Drastically cutting down membership of all other parties (example – Nat. Soc. from 600,000 to 15,000), and replacing existing leaders with communist-approved ones.

Supervised and rigged parliamentary elections with 89% for the CP.

Purges in nationalised companies, civil service, schools, and cultural institutions, dismissing a quarter of a million people from their jobs and sending them to menial work in mines, building sites, and agriculture.

Over 10,500 students expelled from univesities and colleges, mostly on the basis of denouncements by communist fellow students who preside over the expulsions.

Monetary reform which wipes out everybody's savings to make everybody start again penniless.

Deliberate shortages of basic goods, including food.

Punitive taxes on small enterprises which put them out of business and make them join co-operatives or offer their assets for nationalisation.

Law for the protection of the republic No. 231 which serves as a basis for political trials.

Some 230,000 people tried and sentenced under this law in the coming decade.

First 14 executions and 52 life imprisonment sentences passed in 1950, more to follow.

Soviet advisors for "the struggle against class enemies" arriving in autumn 1949.

Whoever is suspect but cannot be proved to be an enemy is branded a "cocooned enemy", which is enough to have him, if not jailed, then certainly transferred to mining or building work.

The entire Czechoslovak ice-hockey team which won the world cup in 1949 is arrested and jailed before departure for the 1950 cup, on suspicion of planning to defect. Czechoslovakia stays out the championship until a new national team can be found for the Winter Olympics 1952, politically reliable enough to lose against the newcomer Soviet team which had been trained for several years by the very Czech players who are now in jail.

And in a final twist of irony, "class enemies" are found inside the top leadership of the Communist Party and 11 death sentences are passed in the notorious "Slansky gang" trial, with hundreds more communists jailed. Some of the executed are Party officials directly responsible for starting the persecution machine in 1948.

Feeling betrayed again by the same President to whom they gladly relegated all responsibility for their own lives, deprived of the last remnant of hope and the last dark corner to run into and hide in, the not so brave ones waive even a pretense of civic decency with a desparate shrug of folk wisdom, "if you can't beat them, join them", and "the darkest place is just under the candlestick". Within a few weeks, a million little red stars glitter on the lapels of teachers, actors, writers, office workers – and shopkeepers, restaurateurs, hair-dressers, shoemakers, and other small entrepreneurs, once the backbone of democracy, now proudly joining the triumphant proletariat destined by historical necessity to rule forever.

Denouncing neighbours and colleagues becomes popular once again, only done with a much greater verve and even a feeling of righteousness which people successfully con themselves into. It is all right this time, this time we are denouncing colleagues for the sake of "the people". Not because we want to get their jobs. Or just get even with the smug bastards. Oh, no. It's socialist justice we care about.

The Scout organisation is disbanded and its leaders jailed as Anglo-American spies. It is replaced by a Party-run children's association called the Pioneers. School children are marched into potato fields to clear them of the Colorado beetle, the epitome of Western evil, sent by the wicked American imperialists to destroy socialist agriculture. The real cause was, of course, the collectivisation which destroyed the ridges separating the fields, thus exterminating partridges and quails which nested there and fed on the beetle. Even children's favourite cartoon hero Ferda the Ant goes into battle with a lance on the back of a green locust, shouting "Go home you evil imperialist beetle!" A few months later, the Ferda series is discontinued and the author jailed when Ferda's peaceful and friendly patch of land is invaded by a gang of evil red ants. Children are regularly asked in school if their parents disagree with anything they are taught. Some innocently denounced parents end in jail.

Culture and education are marxified, and well run by a once respected but by now gaga arts critic and professor with the improbable name of Nejedlý, which translates as Inedible. Popular culture grafitti begin to appear demanding "more edible and less Inedible". One of his great achievements is making a national hero of Smetana – the meaningful national composer, while consigning Dvořák – the meaningless cosmopolitan, to virtual oblivion. Malicious tongues recall that the true reason for this is that young Nejedlý once asked Dvořák for his daughter's hand and was kicked out the door.

The country's great rhymers, having exhausted their measure of socialist enthusiasm, shut up because there's no market for anything else. A few commit suicide, many more drink themselves into kidney and liver colics, as booze remains cheap throughout the communist era. The last thing communist rulers want Czechs to be is sober. A new enthusiastic generation of poets grows to appreciate the creative scope offered by lucrative socialist song-writing, one of whose best examples translates like this:

Time has matured and smells of hope
Streams of sunshine cascade from the clouds
Forward comrades toward the promised land
Where bosses and beggars are no more
Flock our hearts together
Let all join in one faith
Man next to man, hip next to hip
We shall arrive
We shall arrive
The time has come for each of us
To lift his arm and act
Forward left, forward left
Not a step back

Another hit has this youthful poetic message:

Blue and white parades of men and women
Red scarves of the Pioneer children
Young is he who, young is he who
Fights for a happy life
With the army of peace
Young is a poet who sings for the young
Young is a song the pure dove
We are all young, are all young
Young is every communist

But the top prize must surely go to this evergreen which no one who lived at that time can ever forget:

It is I, young freedom blossoming red
It is I, young freedom blossoming red
It is I, young freedom blossoming red
It is I, young freedom blossoming red.

There is, to be fair, a different tune on each of these lines. The second movement goes like this:

It is I, young freedom blossoming red
It is I, young freedom blossoming red
It is I, young freedom blossoming red
It is I, young freedom blossoming red

Pure genius of simplicity. These splendid works of poetic art, written to punchy marching tunes, do precisely what they are designed to: Turn the nation dizzy, tipsy, amnesic, anaesthetised – and malleable. So much so that a decade later, even the most dissatisfied and persecuted find it hard to imagine that the world could be anything other than socialist.

\*\*\*

## August – 21st, 1968

No wonder that when a whiff of freedom appears, the best they can think of is trying to humanise socialism. Of course, being still firmly in the Soviet grip, there's nothing much more they could think of, even if they wanted to. But this gives a great boost to all socialist and left-wing movements throughout Western Europe, to whom the Prague Spring is proof that, yes, didn't we always say so, socialism is principally a humanist idea which works if only it were not corrupted by bureaucrats and power hungry people.

They watch with joy and pride the first ever communist leader daring to take a stroll in the streets without bodyguards, stop for a sausage in Wenceslas Square, go for a swim in a local swimming pool, and give his audiences not the proverbial dictatorial wave of the hand but a symbolic hug.

Yes, Alexander Dubček is the world's pet and hero. And while everyone in the West calls him "the Czech leader", Czechs notice with pleasant surprise that they are, for the first time, enjoying the rule of a Slovak. We and the Slovaks are one now. The man looks like he loves us. Let's love him in return. And an unbelievable love affair breaks out between the long discredited Communist Party and the people of Czechoslovakia. Czechs have always had short memories, a passion for forgiveness, and rose-coloured glasses to see the world with.

A host of human-looking, freedom-professing, intelligent, and above all well-meaning people gather around Dubček to explain the Party's new policies to the re-awakened but suspicious nation. And witty, my God, are they witty in their ad-lib public discussions.

"Will we be able to go to live and work in the West if we want to?"

"More than that, my friend. If we want to, we will be able to live and work even in our own country now."

Smart, huh?

In their enthusiasm for these new elegant and eloquent humanist communists, people fail or refuse to notice that these are the same old bastards who got them into the mess in the first place. Almost every one of them a Stalinist fifteen years ago. Almost every one of them had maligned, denounced, persecuted someone in the revolutionary fervour which followed Triumphant February. Or had written those revolutionary poems and songs.

"Yes, well, we are aware we made a lot of mistakes." (Mistakes, indeed.) "We realise it is our responsibility to put them right. Trust us once more."

And to their own surprise, people do. In the last twenty years, they have learned to trust no one. Trusting someone at long last again is a deep craving in their souls. Relegating responsibility to someone else again. Ready to give their family jewels to their new democratic socialist republic, to help the ailing economy. They speak their minds and are listened to. Every opinion is acceptable. As long as it remains self-censored, self-restricted, socialist. Of course it does. No one knows anything else, no one imagines anything else. You no longer have to be a Party member to be promoted to a responsible job, or work in the media. You don't have to, really. So new young, well-meaning people are joining. It is a democratic party after all now. We don't have to join. So let's.

An unwritten but well understood and deeply felt deal is worked out. We shall allow you this, that, and the other, if you don't do that, the other, and this. You can travel to the West if you help us improve the country's image there. Of course we will, the West loves us anyway, let's just be lovable and tell everyone what a wonderful country we have. You can write what you like, say what you like, ask what you like, provided the argument remains within the parameters of Marxist socialism. Of course it will, we don't know anything else. You can criticise us as much as you like, but please be careful not to attack the Soviet Union.

Ouch.

The trouble is, where do you draw the line? Can you avoid implicating the Soviet Union in the crimes of the Czech communist judiciary of the fifties? But can you afford not to investigate the crimes of the fifties when they are such a good yarn everybody's after? Or should you rather shut up about it? But what do you write about when people are so hungry for information that they buy six papers every day not to miss a damned thing? And, by the way, how was it exactly with Jan Masaryk's defenestration? Wasn't the Soviet Embassy involved?

The first strong warning Dubček gets is in April.

"Be careful lad, there's counter-revolution smoldering under your bed," say the leaders of the Warsaw Pact countries at a joint meeting which he failed to attend.

"Nuts. What counter-revolution? Come and have some fun," is the gist of his reply.

And on he goes, carried away by his popularity, listening to everyone, loving everyone, and trying to make everyone happy, loving, and beautiful. Everyone is, the spring is warm, the summer even warmer, and many new babies are conceived. Every self-respecting Western socialist visits Prague to breathe the air of freedom, love, and uninhibited sex. The hip sixties make gentle Prague, not furious Paris, their golden crown. For a while the reforming craze spills over to Poland, where it is promptly and efficiently suppressed. We cannot allow this to infect us, protest East German leaders as Czech border towns and villages blast amplified Doctor Zhivago music across the border.

Fired by Dubček's personal enthusiasm and charisma, old entrenched bureaucrats wake up to his rhythm and start doing their jobs better than ever before. Shopkeepers smile at customers and customers thank them, as a seed of market-oriented economic reform is planted, and productivity and quality improve. Western newspapers appear in the streets. People start calling themselves Mr and Mrs, and drop their "comrades". A new president is elected, an elderly army general called Svoboda – which means Freedom. Yes, you remember him well, the one who refused to place the army at Beneš's disposal to defend the country in 1948. Another great loving democrat.

Warsaw Pact leaders repeat their warning in May:

"We are determined to prevent any change to the established socialist order."

Dubček replies by allowing dozens of new organisations to be established, including the revival of Sokols and Scouts, and even two political pressure groups calling themselves The Club of Committed Non-Partisans, and Club 231 consisting of former political prisoners. The two tiny parties of the National Front are discussing their revival, and the Social Democratic Party, swallowed up by the communists and dissolved 20 years earlier, is re-emerging.

In June, the Warsaw Pact armies have a joint exercise in Czechoslovakia and map out everything they need for an imminent invasion. No one seems to worry much. Newspapers are awash with details of communist crimes of the fifties and several suicides of their perpetrators follow. The Secret Police splits into two camps – one dancing with the people, the other, knowing this can not go on beyond the apple-picking season, watching and putting together detailed files on all those who have shown themselves publicly to be a danger to the socialist family of nations.

A pamphlet called "The 2000-word Statement" appears in the press, demanding that the reform process must continue even if it jeopardises the leading role of the Communist Party. This tickles the big bear beyond a giggle. The big Warsaw Pact boys meet in Warsaw in July and agree on what becomes known as the Brezhnev Doctrine – the duty of communist parties to defend a sister party whenever it is in danger of losing control.

Another warning letter by the other five (Rumania stays out of this), is turned down by Prague as nonsense, and a meeting is arranged at the Soviet border between the two countries' leaders, which Dubček probably still believes is a friendly tea party to exchange jokes. The same at two more warning meetings with the East German and Hungarian chiefs.

And when Dubček dances his way into Madame Tusseaud's, jealous Brezhnev has had it. On August 20, just before midnight, endless streams of huge aircraft begin to land at the Prague airport and 750,000 Warsaw Pact troops and 6,000 tanks invade Czechoslovakia, and everybody is shocked and surprised.

"How could they do this to me?" gasps Dubček himself, having had a dozen clear warnings that precisely this is what they will do.

Prague Radio stays on the air instead of going off at midnight as usual. During the night, it was meant to be taken over by broadcasters of a new pro-Soviet government which is waiting in the wings. At five a.m., the nation would wake up and be told that a peaceful hand-over saved them from counter-revolution.

The cock-up happened as follows:

The invasion is planned to start after midnight when radio is off the air. The planners, who were timing themselves under summer time in East Germany and Poland, forgot that Czechoslovakia remains under constant Central European time throughout the year. Invaders' midnight is 11 pm in Prague. This mistake triggers off what becomes professionally and politically the most spectacular broadcasting week of all time, and one great inventive peaceful resistance show in which everyone joins with joy.

"Wake up your neighbours and tell them to switch us on," repeats Prague radio every fifteen minutes throughout the crucial night, between reports of the invasion's progress, and names of the quislings who "asked for comradely assistance" of the Soviet Union, but who are now forced by the turn of events to lie low. By 3 am, streets of every town teem with people taking down street signs and direction indicators throughout the country. Whole columns of Warsaw

Pact armies lose their bearings for several days. Trains with Soviet troops and equipment are re-routed by Czech railwaymen and run around the country in circles.

By the time Soviet soldiers take the Prague Radio building late morning of 21 August, dozens of clandestine radio and TV studios are set up throughout the country, each broadcasting in short intervals so that they cannot be detected. This goes on for a week, during which the country, whose leaders have been kidnapped to Moscow, is effectively governed by a couple of hundred sleepless, unshaven, and unwashed broadcasters. Transistor radios are the hottest sale of the week. Radio Luxemburg, the most listened to station in the country, changes its programme to solemn music and broadcasts news on Czechoslovakia every half hour.

Uganda is the first country to present a UN protest against the invasion. By the end of the first day, Czechs have their first invasion joke:

The Entebbe government phones the Kremlin:

"We have your ambassador here to dinner, and if you don't get out of Czechoslovakia now, we shall eat him."

And while people are being machine-gunned and run over by tanks in Prague and other cities, jokes are cheering the nation up to help it carry on:

Corporal Alyosha returns home from his invasion of Czechoslovakia, and his wife asks:

"Nu, show me what new you have learned from those counter-revolutionaries."

Alyosha takes a piece of chalk, draws a line in the middle of the hut, and says:

"Nu vot, this is where we shall sleep, this is where we shall shit."

191

Jokes of the powerless, but jokes nevertheless.

The bullet-sprayed facade of Prague Museum displays a poster:

"The Art of El Grechko" (General Grechko being the Soviet chief commander.)

This becomes the proudest week in the nation's modern history, as they surprise themselves by their resolve and unprecedented unity. They have prevented the establishment of a quisling government and forced Brezhnev to return their kidnapped leaders back alive, if somewhat dishevelled. The people, who haven't slept for a week, sigh with relief when they see Dubček appear on TV, a small plaster on his forehead, thanking the people for sticking by their leaders, and in effect saving their lives.

As a reward for their support, he presents his people a "normalisation" treaty which all of the leaders, except one Spanish Civil War veteran, have signed in Moscow. Soviet troops are to stay indefinitely. The media is to come under censorhip, some key personnel to be replaced. The present leadership will stay in office to modify the effects of the treaty, pledging to go on pursuing some of the reforms. By now, his listeners are reading between his lines, and when he says "I personally will not blame anyone who does not wish to stay", a Czechoslovak invasion of Western embassies breaks out and half a million people leave. They have 7 months to make up their minds, before Dubček and his boys are replaced.

This emigration consists 70% of young people, many of them graduates or highly skilled. Most of these do not go into exile to fight but to forget. They've had enough of their country. They want freedom, fully-fledged freedom which they can take for granted, for themselves and their children, without socialism, without a human face. They leave their homes to become loyal Canadians, Australians, Americans, Swiss, Brits, Frenchmen, Scandinavians, Germans and Austrians. Most of them succeed, and most of their children do not learn Czech.

Back home, a human torch named Jan Palach burns in Wenceslas Square in January 1969, followed by a second one a week later. The previous year's reforms are stalled and abandoned, a centralised economy reinstated. Soviet leadership complains that the normalisation is proceeding too slowly, and more hard-liners are placed in executive positions in the Party and the government.

And then comes the final straw. The Czechoslovak ice-hockey team beats the Soviets at the world cup, and elated Czech TV viewers take to the streets. The event turns into a spontaneous anti-Soviet demonstration during which Aeroflot and other Soviet offices are damaged. The only thing that could bring the Czechs to heel is a full-scale repression, which starts within days.

All reform communists are chucked out of the Party, government, parliament, National Front parties, army, and police. During the year to come, some 30,000 people will lose their jobs. Almost 20% of army officers will be purged, and almost one third of secret police officers who supported the Prague Spring. Universities, schools and academic institutions will lose 25% of teachers, scientists and researchers. In one university, the departments of English, German, French, and Romanesque languages will lose so many teachers that the remnant will have to be combined into a single Department of Western Languages, with only an Associate Professor at its head.

In April 1969, Dubček is sent to Turkey as ambassador in the hope that he will defect (he doesn't), and the top Party job goes to another Slovak, Gustáv Husák.

A survivor of the prison camps in the fifties, rehabilitated with honours, climbing up the reformist ladder in the sixties, Husák turns around in 1969 to preside over the dullest, drabbest, most idiotic, most loyal and subdued regime in the Soviet block, in which Czechs and Slovaks are buried alive in cultural oblivion, economic corruption and moral, mental, and environmental devastation. The nation's skills and talents are used to make Czechoslovakia famous for three things: arms sales to every anti-democratic regime on the planet, training of terrorists, and semtex.

To the Western world, the Soviet invasion has done a great service: It has cured their communists and socialists of their last illusions of any humanist values and principles in socialism, and ushered in an era of old-fashioned democratic conservatism, which sticks to its guns until communism collapses after a series of Regan-Gorbachov poker games.

\*\*\*

## November – 17th, 1989

And freedom falls on the Czechs again without a fistfight, except for a couple of hundred students beaten up by police truncheons.

A Secret Police KGB-inspired operation named "Wedge" goes into action to participate in the overthrow of the sclerotic regime and plant its agents in every new democratic movement and organisation which crops up, as well as in positions of economic and financial power. How deeply entrenched they become in what gradually begins to resemble a normal democratic political spectrum, or how powerful they remain to control it, is an issue which has been debated by journalists and suspected by many citizens, but

JE TO PARADOX
SVATÝ VÁCLAVE
HILFE !
EX·LIBRIS

HELP US, VÁCLAV HAVEL!

will probably never be conclusively documented. Too many files have disappeared.

And most Czechs don't care, and don't want to know. As always, their memory is short, their desire to forgive strong. Above all, their craving for comfort overrides everything else, and they do feel more comfortable than they have for a very long time. They want to be left to themselves, develop their talents and skills to their best ability and marketability, let their long suppressed entrepreneurial drive explode. They want to stop being bothered by politics and who's who.

They have more registered private entrepreneurs, small companies, and small shareholders per capita than any other country in Europe. In most surveys, some 70% claim to be better off than before, and less than 10% feel life was better under communism. They have the highest GDP of all the post-communist countries. The lowest unemployment rate in Europe of under 3%, industrial relations in good shape, social peace. A steadily growing private sector. Annual growth of around 5%. A sharp annual increase in overall private income and personal purchasing power. The first post communist country with a stable and convertible currency. The highest incoming foreign investment of all post-communist countries. An international credit rating overtaking Mexico, Venezuela, Greece and Turkey in 1995, on a par with Israel and just behind Portugal. One hundred million – yes, that is 100,000,000 – incoming foreign tourist border crossings a year, even though that figure includes border region Germans coming for an evening beer.

At the same time, crooks have never known a greater bonanza, and are making the best of it – with impunity.

Once again, the great image-builders that the Czechs are have become everybody's favourite pet.

196

But six years after the fall of communism, it is still by no means decided whether the Czech Republic is on its way to becoming a true Western democracy, as craved by most of its people and hoped for by its Western fans, or a mafia-controlled market economy with corruptible officials on every step of the political, judiciary, and economic ladder, and across the political spectrum, where election results are irrelevant, Latin American style.

But once again, they are determined to make it to the top.

By hook or by crook, they will probably get there.

Provided they don't screw up again.

Thomas Garrigue Masaryk once said that a state lives and survives by the idea on which it was created.

So it does.

What's the idea?